Quran is perfect and infallible.

Abdul-Razzaq

TABLE OF CONTENTS

ABSTRACT

Qur'anic Inerrancy is the idea that the Qur'an has been given by an omnipotent and omniscient God and therefore has no errors whatsoever in its text, and that this text has been perfectly preserved since the time of its revelation. This concept is widely held throughout the Muslim community. The traditional Islamic account of the collection of the Qur'an has issues that lead to doubts regarding its authenticity. Vowel marking, memory research, and the seven *ahruf* all lead to questions regarding the validity of the theory of Qur'anic inerrancy. Variant texts, including those immediately copied from the Uthman's Qur'an, as well as by respected experts on the Qur'an, lead to suspicion of the effectiveness and correctness of Uthman's standardization. Specific instances within the Qur'an, such as the belief that the people of Gog and Magog are currently imprisoned behind a wall created by Alexander the Great, bode very poorly for the belief in Qur'anic inerrancy. Qur'anic inerrancy and similar forms of scriptural literalism may have a substantial impact on a religion's longevity and widespread societal acceptance. The presence of errors within a holy text lead to the question of how many mistakes should be acceptable before the associated religion's validity is questioned.

INTRODUCTION

Qur'anic Inerrancy is the idea that the Qur'an has been given by an omnipotent and omniscient God and therefore has no errors whatsoever in its text, and that this text has been perfectly preserved since the time of its revelation. This concept is widely held throughout the Muslim community. Some Muslims describe the Qur'an as "immaculately preserved"[1] and "the Word of Allāh, constant, immaculate, unalterable, inimitable".[2] According to this theory, the contents of the Qur'an should be perfect and not contain a single error or mistake. This book will examine the background and topics associated with the theory of Qur'anic inerrancy, and after examining the evidence I will discuss whether this theory is logical. I will also analyze the effect errors in scripture may have on societal acceptance of the associated religion. I will also briefly discuss the role of reason in relation to errant holy texts and their respective religions.

Ibn Warraq states: "For the average, unphilosophical Muslim of today, the Koran remains the infallible word of God, the immediate word of God sent down… in perfect, pure Arabic; and every thing contained therein is eternal and uncreated… Modern Muslims also claim that these revelations have been preserved exactly as revealed to Muhammad, without any change, addition, or loss whatsoever."[3] Muslim scholars, such as M.M. Al-Azami, attest to the inerrancy of the Qur'an as well, "The Qur'ān is the very word of Allāh, His final message to all humanity, revealed to His final messenger Muhammad and transcending all limitations of time and space. It is preserved in its original tongue without any amendments, additions, or deletions."[4]

---

[1] M.M. Al-Azami. *The History of the Qu'rānic Text: from Revelation to Compilation: A Comparative Study with the Old and New Testaments* (Leicester: UK Islamic Academy, 2003) 149.

[2] Ibid., 343.

[3] Ibn Warraq. *Why I Am Not A Muslim.* 2nd Ed (N.p.: Momus and Warraq Publishers, LLC, 2020) 105.

[4] Azami, *The History*, 13.

Unlike the Bible which is seen by many Christians as being the words of humans (albeit through the influence of the Holy Spirit), the Qur'an is seen as the actual word of God given to Muhammed through the angel Gabriel. Therefore, it is typically Allah speaking in the text. While the position of biblical inerrancy is very common among conservative and fundamentalist Christians, the belief in Qur'anic inerrancy is likely even higher among the general Muslim population. Ibn Warraq describes it this way, "we can legitimately distinguish between fundamentalist and nonfundamentalist Christians, [but], … all Muslims—not just a group called 'fundamentalist'—believe that the Koran is the word of God."[5]

The basis for the idea of inerrancy comes from a variety of verses in the Qur'an. Qur'an 18:1-2 reads: "[All] praise is [due] to Allāh, who has sent down upon His Servant [Muḥammad (ﷺ)] the Book and has not made therein any deviance. [He has made it] straight, to warn of severe punishment from Him and to give good tidings to the believers who do righteous deeds that they will have a good reward [i.e., Paradise]."[6] Q 15:9 says: "Indeed, it is We who sent down the message [i.e., the Qur'ān], and indeed, We will be its guardian."[7] As Ingrid Mattson states: "Muslim scholars interpret this as a promise from God that nothing of the Qur'an that was revealed to the Prophet Muhammad could ever be lost or changed."[8]

The Qur'an contains its own test in order to determine the authenticity of its contents. Q 2:23-24: "And if you are in doubt about what We have sent down [i.e., the Qur'ān] upon Our Servant [i.e., Prophet Muḥammad (ﷺ)], then produce a sūrah the like thereof and call upon your witnesses [i.e., supporters] other than Allāh, if you should be truthful. But if you do not - and you

---

[5] Ibn Warraq, *Why I*, 11.

[6] Qur'an 18:1-2 (Saheeh International)

[7] Qur'an 15:9 (SI)

[8] Ingrid Mattson. *The Story of the Qur'an: Its History and Place in Muslim Life* (N.p.: Blackwell Publishing, 2008) 96-97.

will never be able to - then fear the Fire, whose fuel is people and stones, prepared for the disbelievers."[9] This test challenges a person to try to imitate the Qur'an and to match the elegance of its words, the failure to do so is seen as proof of the Qur'an's divine authorship. The Qur'an even claims that not even a single sura could be imitated by a human.

In this book, I will examine the theory that the Qur'an is inerrant and perfectly accurate. In Chapter One, I will be examining the formation of the Qur'an. This section will look at the traditional Islamic account of how the Qur'an was put together, as well as information that challenges this account. I will also examine other related topics such as the seven readings and the seven *ahruf*. In Chapter Two, I will be looking at the views that different Islamic groups and Muslim scholars have held regarding Qur'anic inerrancy throughout history. I will also explore variant texts, including those by prominent Qur'anic experts. Chapter Three will be an examination of specific examples that will help to argue for or against the inerrancy of the Qur'an. In this section, I will look at topics such as historicity, inconsistencies, prophecies, and miracles that are within the Qur'an to help study the validity of the claim of Qur'anic inerrancy. Chapter Four will look at whether inerrancy is explicitly stated within the Qur'an, and if inerrancy is necessary for Islam and other faiths. I will also look at the line between religion and mythology and the role that scriptural inerrancy plays in determining individual and societal views regarding the legitimacy of religion.

The Scope of The book and Other Notes

The theory of Qur'anic inerrancy covers a wide variety of different topics such as variant Qur'anic texts, Qur'anic manuscripts, the history of the Qur'an's collection, orthography, the seven *ahruf,* and more. To cover them all in detail would be outside the scope of this work.

---

[9] Qur'an 2:23-24 (SI)

Therefore, enough information will be provided to give a general understanding of Qur'anic inerrancy and the major topics that impact this theory.

The only version of the Qur'an that is considered by Muslims to be the exact words of Allah is in the Arabic language. Qur'an 39:28 reads: "[It is] an Arabic Qur'ān, without any deviance that they might become righteous."[10] Most Muslims consider any non-Arabic translation to be a lesser form of the original Arabic word of God. Therefore, while the English translations included in this work will give a good idea of the contents of the Qur'an and the arguments based on them, the exact wording of the Arabic is slightly different due to translation.

There are different definitions for the term "Islamic scholar". This book will use the term "Islamic scholar" to mean an individual who studies Islam regardless of their personal religious views. "Muslim scholar" will be used to distinguish a person who is a scholar of Islam and who also believes in the religion of Islam.

History of Scholarship

The concept of Qur'anic inerrancy is covered in part by many authors, however, to list every author that impacts this topic would be nearly impossible. Instead, this History of Scholarship will cover authors who focus primarily on Qur'anic inerrancy, as well as notable authors who have sections that significantly contribute to the discussion of the topic. Relevant areas include variant Qur'anic texts, Qur'anic manuscripts, the history of the Qur'an's collection, the seven *ahruf*, orthography, and more.

Solomon Schimmel's book *The Tenacity of Unreasonable Belief: Fundamentalism and the Fear of Truth* is one of the few works that focuses specifically on scriptural inerrancy. Schimmel was motivated by his upbringing in orthodox Judaism and what he eventually saw as the unlikely belief in the inerrancy of certain Jewish writings. His original focus was only on

---

[10] Qur'an 39:28 (SI). Other verses that talk about the Qur'an being revealed in Arabic include Q 12:2 and Q 16:103.

these Jewish writings, however, his work expanded to include biblical and Qur'anic inerrancy. As can be inferred from the title of the book, as well as the cover image (a bird with its head buried in the sand), it is clear that Schimmel does not find arguments of scriptural inerrancy to be convincing in either Judaism, Christianity, or Islam. Schimmel talks about possible examples of errors, variant texts, abrogation, the inimitability of the Qur'an, and more. He also comments on the relationship between faith and reason. Schimmel's book is the only credible resource that was found that deals almost exclusively with scriptural inerrancy. While the book does not focus solely on Qur'anic inerrancy it is a valuable resource in understanding "scriptural fundamentalist beliefs".[11]

Ibn Warraq has written a variety of books that criticize Islam, especially fundamentalist views. His book *Why I Am Not a Muslim* addresses a variety of different topics within Islam including the inerrancy of the Qur'an. Ibn Warraq is a pseudonym, as the author was influenced by the Rushdie Affair, and saw his views as having the potential to bring threats against his life. Ibn Warraq comments on a wide variety of perceived issues such as the first-person speech of Allah, variant texts, historical errors in the Qur'an, syntax errors in the Qur'an, as well as historical Islamic views including rationalist tendencies by groups such as the Mutazilites. Ibn Warraq also discusses other topics such as homophobia, women's rights, the earliest biographies of Muhammad, the hadiths, and much more. Ibn Warraq comments on the unreliability of the early Islamic accounts including issues with the traditional Islamic narrative regarding the collection of the Qur'an. While *Why I Am Not a Muslim* does not deal exclusively with Qur'anic inerrancy, it includes this discussion as well as comments on many other subjects that have a

---

[11] Solomon Schimmel. *The Tenacity of Unreasonable Beliefs: Fundamentalism and the Fear of Truth.* (Oxford: Oxford University Press, 2008) 4. https://web-p-ebscohost-com.athens.idm.oclc.org/ehost/ebookviewer/ebook/bmxlYmtfXzI0MjE4N19fQU41?sid=18fe58be-d41f-4354-acf8-9ba0e1ea7058@redis&vid=0&format=EB&rid=1

direct impact on Qur'anic inerrancy. Ibn Warraq also has other books on Qur'anic studies such as *The Origins of the Koran* (1998) and *Which Koran?* (2011)

Many early Muslim scholars from the 7th century C.E. and on, discuss a wide variety of topics that impact inerrancy. These topics include inerrancy specifically, the history of the collection of the Qur'an, variant texts, orthography, *I'jaz* (the inimitability of the Qur'an), the seven *ahruf* of the Qur'an, and more. While there are certainly those who disagree with the claim of inerrancy, most of the Muslim scholars throughout the history of Islam have defended the inerrancy of the Qur'an. These Muslim scholars will be covered in more detail in Chapter Two.

Theodor Nöldeke is considered one of the fathers of Western Islamic Studies and is probably cited more than any other Western scholar due to his impact on the field. His works include "The Koran," published in Encyclopaedia Britannica in 1891, and *Geschichte des Qorâns* [History of the Koran] (1860). While his writings are not focused specifically on Qur'anic inerrancy, the topics he covers are heavily associated with the subject. These topics include speech other than by Allah, syntax errors, variant texts, the seven *ahruf*, abrogation, the incorrect identity of Miriam, and more. His work directly impacts the study of Qur'anic inerrancy as well as Islam in general.

Ignaz Goldziher is another early Orientalist scholar still cited heavily among Orientalists and Muslims today. His paper "On the Development of the Hadith" focuses on the hadith collections rather than the Qur'an. His conclusions revealed that many hadiths that are considered "sound" are not reliable and that they may have been influenced by political and social pressures at the time of their writing. Goldziher's writings are heavily criticized by Muslim scholars. Goldziher's writings on the hadith are relevant to the study of Qur'anic inerrancy as many early accounts of the Qur'an's collection are found in the hadith literature. There is also other relevant information found in the hadiths such as on variant texts, the seven *ahruf*, and more.

Julius Wellhausen, Leone Caetani, and Henri Lammens questioned the authenticity of certain Muslim traditions. This includes Caetani and Lammens doubts about the biographies of Muhammad, known as *sīra*, many of which provide information about the early years of Islam and the collection of the Qur'an.[12] Their findings suggest that early Muslim writers may have been more interested in constructing "an ideal vision of the past" than a realistic one.[13] Caetani in "'Uthman and the Recension of the Koran" comments on the traditional Islamic account of the collection of the Qur'an. Lammens works include: "*Scripta Pontificii Instituti Biblica*"

Alphonse Mingana's works include *Leaves from Three Ancient Qurâns Possibly Pre-'Othmânic with a List of their Variants* and "The Transmission of the Koran." Mingana examines different variants in the text such as word choice and possible scribal errors. He also comments on inconsistencies in the text including the identity of Miriam and Haman.[14] Other topics discussed by Mingana include abrogation, syntax, history of the vowel markings, and memory research. He also comments that audiences do not know which verses came from Zaid's memory and which came from written sources during the collection of the Qur'an.[15]

Ali Dashti's *Twenty Three Years: A Study of the Prophetic Career of Mohammad* is a book that was written in 1937, but was not published until 1974.[16] The book was likely published in Beirut as the Shah of Iran did not allow publications that were critical of religion between 1971 and 1977.[17] In this book Dashti "defends rational thought in general and criticizes blind

---

[12] Ibn Warraq, ed. *The Origins of the Koran: Classic Essays on Islam's Holy Book* (Amherst, NY: Prometheus Books, 1998) 19.

[13] Ibid.

[14] Alphonse Mingana. "Three Ancient Korans," in Ibn Warraq, ed. *The Origins of the Koran: Classic Essays on Islam's Holy Book* (Amherst, NY: Prometheus Books, 1998) 79.

[15] Ibid., 82.

[16] Ibn Warraq, *Why I*, 4.

[17] Ibid.

faith".[18] He strongly denies any of the miracles attributed to Muhammed, and is skeptical about the orthodox view that the Qur'an is the word of God and that it is miraculous.[19] He also questions the claimed eloquence of the Qur'an.[20] He says of some Muslim scholars that 'before bigotry and hyperbole prevailed, [they] openly acknowledged that the arrangement and syntax of the Koran are not miraculous and that work of equal or greater value could be produced by other God-fearing persons'.[21] He also criticized the Qur'an due to its foreign words, and the confusion of the identities of God and Muhammed as the speaker.[22] After spending three years in Khomeini's prisons, and after being tortured even at the age of 83, Dashti died in 1984.[23]

Arthur Jeffery's works include *The Qur'ān as Scripture*, *Materials for the History of the Text of the Qur'ān: The Old Codices*[24], "Progress in the Study of the Koran Text," and "Abu 'Ubaid on the Verses Missing from the Koran" (1938). Jeffery wrote on a variety of relevant topics, including his prominent work on textual variants. He criticizes the story of Abu Bakr's official recension and believes that its authenticity is doubtful.[25] Jeffery also commented on possible detractors from Uthman's codex such as Shanabudh and Ibn Masud. He notes: "It is very significant that the *Qurra'* were violently opposed to 'Uthman because of this act, and there is evidence that for quite a while the Muslims in Kufa were divided into two factions, those who

---

[18] Ibid.

[19] Ibid.

[20] Ibid.

[21] Ali Dashti. *Twenty-Three Years: A Study of the Prophetic Career of Mohammed* (London, 1985), 10. Quoted in Ibn Warraq, *Why I Am Not A Muslim.* 2nd Ed (N.p.: Momus and Warraq Publishers, LLC, 2020), 4.

[22] Dashti, *Twenty-Three Years*, 50. Quoted in Ibn Warraq, *Why I*, 4-5.; Ibn Warraq, *Why I*, 5.

[23] Ibn Warraq, *Why I*, 5.

[24] This work was edited by Jeffery.

[25] Arthur Jeffery. "Materials for the History of the Text of the Koran," in Ibn Warraq, ed. *The Origins of the Koran: Classic Essays on Islam's Holy Book* (Amherst, NY: Prometheus Books, 1998) 117.

accepted the 'Uthmanic text, and those who stood by Ibn Mas'ud, who had refused to give up his codex to be burned."[26] He also notes that "say" was probably added to verses to remedy issues with Allah's first-person speech. Jeffery states:

> That our present text of the Koran represents an honest effort to assemble all that was still extent of genuine proclamations of Muhammed during the years of his prophetic activity need not be questioned. It is possible but not very probable that a few passages have crept in which are not genuine proclamations of the Prophet. That a great many quite genuine proclamations, however, could no longer be found, and are thus not included in the volume, is certain.[27]

Richard Bell and William Montgomery Watt in the work *Introduction to the Qur'ān* question many grammatical and syntax issues such as "breaks in grammatical construction which raise difficulties in exegesis", "juxtaposition of apparently contrary statements", and more.[28] Watt accepts the story of the Satanic Verses saying "Indeed the story is so strange, that it must be true in essentials."[29] Watt believes that "the story of Adam and Eve… has no place in a scientific account of the origins of the human race."[30] He comments on the historicity of certain Islamic traditions such as the idea that Abraham helped create the Kaaba as he believes that "Abraham

---

[26] Ibid., 118.

[27] Arthur Jeffery. "Abu 'Ubaid on the Verses Missing from the Koran," in Ibn Warraq, ed. *The Origins of the Koran: Classic Essays on Islam's Holy Book* (Amherst, NY: Prometheus Books, 1998) 150.

[28] R. Bell and W.M. Watt. *Introduction to the Quran* (Edinburgh, 1970) 93. Quoted in Ibn Warraq, ed. *The Origins of the Koran: Classic Essays on Islam's Holy Book* (Amherst, NY: Prometheus Books, 1998) 17.

[29] W. Montgomery Watt. *Muhammad Prophet and Statesman* (Oxford University Press, 1961) 61. Quoted in M. R. Kazimi. *Revisionist History of Islam: A Critical Study of Post 1977 Interpretations* (Karach, Pakistan: SAMA, 2017) 61.

[30] W. Montgomery Watt. *Muslim-Christian Encounters* (London, 1991) 134-135. Quoted in Ibn Warraq, *Why I Am Not A Muslim.* 2nd Ed. (N.p.: Momus and Warraq Publishers, LLC, 2020) 134

never reached Mecca."[31] Watt appears to admire Muhammed and is less critical of Islamic expansionism compared to other Islamic scholars.[32]

John Wansbrough worked at the School of Oriental and African Studies at the University of London. He is one of the most famous Orientalists and influenced others such as Patricia Crane and Michael Cook. His writings include *Quranic Studies: Sources and Methods of Scriptural Interpretation* and *The Sectarian Milieu: Content and Composition of Islamic Salvation History*. He wrote on many topics that are related to Qur'anic inerrancy. Wansbrough suggested that the hadiths and the Qur'an are a "community product spanning two centuries which were then fictitiously attributed to an Arabian prophet based on Jewish prototypes".[33] "Wansbrough shows that far from being fixed in the seventh century, the definitive text of the Koran had still not been achieved as late as the ninth century".[34] He suggests that Islam arose when Arabs interacted with Rabbinic Judaism.[35]

A group of Soviet Islamists, such as N.A. Morozov, also contributed work that is relevant to Qur'anic inerrancy. N.A. Morozov said, 'until the Crusades Islam was indistinguishable from Judaism and ... only then did it receive its independent character, while Muhammed and the first Caliphs are mythical figures'.[36] The Soviet Islamists built upon the work of others before them such as Caetani and Lammens.[37]

---

[31] Watt, *Muslim-Christian Encounters*, 136. Quoted in Ibn Warraq, *Why I*, 131.

[32] Ibn Warraq, *Why I*, 344-346.

[33] Al-Azami, *The History*, 9.

[34] Ibn Warraq, *The Origins*, 24.

[35] Ibid.

[36] T. Lester. "What is Koran?" *The Atlantic Monthly* 283/1 (January 1999): 44. Quoted in M.M. Al-Azami. *The History of the Qu'rānic Text: from Revelation to Compilation: A Comparative Study with the Old and New Testaments* (Leicester: UK Islamic Academy, 2003) 4.

[37] Ibn Warraq, *The Origins*, 19.

Patricia Crone and Michael Cook have written extensively on the Qur'anic text. While they have individual works they are most widely known for their joint work: *Hagarism: The Making of the Islamic World*. This book heavily questions the historical accuracy of many aspects of the early Muslim accounts, seeing them as being too late and unreliable[38], including the economic and social conditions of Muhammad. Cook, Crone, and Martin Hinds "regard the whole established version of Islamic history down at least to the time of Abd al-Malik (685-705) as a later fabrication, and reconstruct the Arab Conquests and the formation of the Caliphate as a movement of peninsular Arabs who had been inspired by Jewish messianism to try to reclaim the Promised Land."[39] Cook and Crone's writings have been criticized especially among Muslim scholars. Leonard Binder comments: "There is, perhaps no more outrageously antagonistic critique of Islam than that which calls it Hagarism. Patricia Crone and Michael Cook, the inventors of Hagarism".[40]

Andrew Rippin was a professor of Religious Studies at the University of Calgary. He has commented on variant readings of the Qur'an and manuscripts from the early history of the Qur'anic text.[41] He suggests that the "Koran is a kind of cocktail of texts that were not all understood even at the time of Muhammad."[42] He even suggests that some may even be 100 years older than Islam.[43] His works include "Literary Analysis of Koran, Tafsir, and Sira: The Methodologies of John Wansbrough."

---

[38] Ibid., 30.

[39] Ibn Warraq, *Why I*, 76.

[40] Leonard Binder. *Islamic Liberalism: A Critique of Development Ideologies* (Chicago: The University of Chicago Press, 1988) 103.

[41] Lester, "What is Koran?" 45. Quoted in Al-Azami, *The History*, 5.

[42] Lester, "What is Koran?" 46. Quoted in Al-Azami, *The History*, 5.

[43] Ibid.

Aḥmad ʻAlī Al Imām's works include *Variant Readings of the Qur'an: A Critical Study of Their Historical and Linguistic Origins*. While Al Imām's work is not specifically geared towards defending Qur'anic inerrancy, the study of the seven *ahruf* (or seven versions) of the Qur'an is a crucial component used by Muslims for explaining early differences in Qur'anic manuscripts, even after the standardization by Uthman. Al Imām comes from a Muslim point of view and he attempts to defend Muslim interpretations of history.

Yasin Dutton's work "An Early *Muṣhaf* According to the Reading of Ibn ʻĀmir" discusses early Qur'anic manuscripts as well as variants. He also discusses the role of the seven *ahruf* as well as Mujahid's seven readings. In other works, Dutton has discussed Islamic law including some of the sources for its origin. He has also talked about issues related to the vocalization of the Qur'an.

M. M. Al-Azami was a Muslim scholar who wrote on the Qur'anic text and the history of the collection of the Qur'an. His book: *The History of the Qur'ānic Text: from Revelation to Compilation: A Comparative Study with the Old and New Testaments* was written partially in an attempt to answer the challenge made by Toby Lester in his article in *The Atlantic Monthly* (January 1999) which claimed that Muslim were unable to defend the inerrancy of the Qur'an in a scholarly fashion.[44] This work gives details regarding the collection of the Qur'an as well as a defense of certain criticized aspects of the traditional Islamic account. Al-Azami's work is a necessary counterweight compared to Orientalist writings and helped give excellent information regarding the history of the formation of the Qur'anic text.

Stephen J. Shoemaker has written on the Qur'anic text and his work is an interesting and useful tool for understanding Orientalist perspectives on the formation of the text. Shoemaker's works include *Death of a Prophet* and *Creating the Qur'an: A Historical-Critical Study*. Shoemaker heavily criticizes the traditional Islamic collection account under Uthman.

---

[44] Al-Azami, *The History*, Preface.

Shoemaker also argues that findings from memory research as well as the political abilities of the time would not allow the Qur'an to be collected according to the traditional narrative. He also argues that the Qur'an was collected later than traditionally believed under the leadership of 'Abd al-Malik. He believes this is due to the perceived inability of the early caliphs to undertake the task successfully. Shoemaker also discusses research on textual variants including the inscription from the Dome of the Rock as well as coins with variant texts. He also questions the reliability of carbon dating and its use with early manuscripts.

It is rare for an author to specifically examine the theory of Qur'anic inerrancy by comprehensively exploring a majority of the variables that affect this concept. Ibn Warraq is one of the exceptional authors who does this. Solomon Schimmel does examine the broader topic of scriptural literalism, however, he provides only a single chapter in his book *The Tenacity of Unreasonable Belief* dedicated to Qur'anic inerrancy. M.M. Al-Azami attempts to defend Qur'anic inerrancy in his book *The History of the Qur'anic Text*, a book partially motivated by a challenge from Toby Lester. Few authors focus on Qur'anic inerrancy as a whole, however, many authors have contributed to topics that directly impact this concept. This is but a sample of the authors and works that have relevance in the study of Qur'anic inerrancy.[45]

---

[45] Others authors include Charles Adams, Muhammad Asad, James Bellamy, Uwe Bergmann, Gotthelf Bergsträsser, Régis Blachère, Khalid Blankinship, Daniel A. Brubaker, John Burton, Fred Donner, Louay Fatoohi, Gustav Flügel, Alfred Guillaume, Martin Hinds, Hartwig Hirschfeld, C. Snouck Hurgronje, Ibn Kammūna, Judith Koren, Toby Lester, David S. Margoliouth, William Muir, Angelika Neuwirth, Yehuda D. Nevo, Otto Pretzl, Gerd R. Puin, Intisar A. Rabb, Behnam Sadeghi, Shehzad Saleem, Joseph Schacht, Friedrich Schwally, Alford T. Welch, and many others.

CHAPTER ONE

THE FORMATION OF THE QUR'AN

There are a variety of stories and opinions regarding the formation of the Qur'an.

Understanding the traditional Islamic narrative of the formation of the Qur'an is important for

understanding the claim that it is inerrant. However, as the traditional Islamic account has

conflicting reports regarding it, some details are subject to debate. I will also examine some of

the secular opinions regarding the formation of the Qur'an, as well as other relevant information

such as the seven *ahruf*, vowel markings, memory research, and more.

The Traditional Islamic Account of the Collection of the Qur'an

Muhammed was born in the year 570 CE near Mecca, which is in modern-day Saudi

Arabia. He is considered to have been an honest merchant and a respected member of the

community. When he was about 40 years old (around 610 CE), he had a revelation from God in a

cave on the outskirts of Mecca. From this point on he preached the message of Allah and

monotheism, converting a number of people to its cause. The Muslims then moved to Medina

(also known as Yathrib) where they were welcomed by the local population. This is in contrast to

the harsh treatment they received at the hands of the polytheistic Meccans. Over time, the

Muslims conquered Mecca and went on to have incredible military and political success

throughout the Middle East.

Over 23 years, from the time of his first revelation in the cave until his death in 632 C.E.,

Muhammad received revelations from God through the angel Gabriel. Orthodox Muslims believe

that Muhammad would collaborate every year with Gabriel to go over the revelations that had

been revealed to that point, and that they did this twice in the year that Muhammad died.[1] This

---

[1] Jeffery, "Materials for," 116.

was to maintain the accuracy of the revelations of the Qur'an. There are a variety of opinions on whether the Qur'an was written down, either in part or in its entirety, before Muhammad's death. However, the standard view is that the Qur'an had to be collected from various written sources as well as from those who had memorized the words of the Qur'an. This task was completed with the help of the first three caliphs and was ultimately completed by Uthman (ruled 644-656 CE).[2]

The first caliph, Abu Bakr, commanded the collection of the Qur'an after the Battle of Yamama, where many Muslims who had memorized the Qur'an had perished in the fighting. Abu Bakr turned to Zaid ibn Thabit to compile the Qur'an in order to safeguard it.[3] Zaid is considered to have had very strong credentials for the role of collector.[4] It is said that he even lived in the Prophet's neighborhood and that his intelligence, morals, and prior experience with recording meant he was a reliable candidate for the job.[5] Zaid was at first reluctant claiming: "How can we embark on what the Prophet never did?".[6] However, Abu Bakr and Umar convinced Zaid that it was the right course of action.

According to Ibn Hajar: "Zaid was unwilling to accept any written material for consideration unless two Companions bore witness that the man received his dictation from the Prophet himself."[7] According to Muslim scholars such as M.M. Al-Azami, Zaid was very

---

[2] Michael Cook. *The Koran: A Very Short Introduction* (Oxford: Oxford University Press, 2000) 119.

[3] Muhammad b. Ismā'īl Al-Bukhārī. *Sahīh.* 4986. Quoted in M. M. Al-Azami. *The History of the Qu'rānic Text: from Revelation to Compilation: A Comparative Study with the Old and New Testaments* (Leicester: UK Islamic Academy, 2003) 78.

[4] Al-Azami, *The History*, 78-79.

[5] Ibid.

[6] Al-Bukhari, *Sahih*, 4986. Quoted in Al-Azami, *The History*, 78.

[7] Ahmad b. 'Ali Ibn Hajar al-'Asqalani. *Fathul Bari*, ed. F. 'Abdul-Baqi, 13 vols (al-Matba'ah as-Salafiyya, Cairo, 1380-1390) ix:14. Quoted in M. M. Al-Azami. *The History of the Qu'rānic Text: from Revelation to Compilation: A Comparative Study with the Old and New Testaments* (Leicester: UK Islamic Academy, 2003) 80.

conscientious and picky regarding the sources he used, claiming that only first-hand material that was "transcribed under the Prophet's supervision" and accompanied with two witnesses, was used when compiling the Qur'an. [8] It does seem that people's memories were used as well, and that the entire Qur'an was not collected from only written material. [9]

Once the collection of the Qur'an was completed, it "was placed in the 'state archives' under the custodianship of Abu Bakr". [10] Al-Azami claims at this point that all suras and verses were properly organized. [11] The next caliph, Umar (who played a role in the original collection), was entrusted with the Qur'an by Abu Bakr. [12] Umar then gave the collection to Hafsa, the widow of Muhammad.

The third caliph, Uthman, was warned about disagreements arising over different dialects of the Qur'an. [13] At this point, there are two main theories on how Uthman went about completing the task of compiling the Qur'an, and Hafsa plays a role in both stories. [14] The first suggests that Uthman simply copied the Qur'an that was in Hafsa's possession. [15] In the other, Uthman created a committee of 12 people, among which was the original compiler Zaid ibn

---

[8] Al-Azami, *The History*, 82.

[9] Ibid., 83.

[10] Ibid., 84.

[11] Al-Azami, *The History*, 84-85.

[12] Qasim b. Sallam Abu 'Ubaid. *Fada'il al Qur'an*, ed. M. al-'Atiyya *et al* (Damascus, 1415/1995) 281. Quoted in M. M. Al-Azami. *The History of the Qu'rānic Text: from Revelation to Compilation: A Comparative Study with the Old and New Testaments* (Leicester: UK Islamic Academy, 2003) 85.

[13] Al-Azami, *The History*, 88.

[14] Ibid.

[15] Ibid.

Thabit.[16] The committee was instructed that when in doubt about possible variations they should use the Quraishi dialect, and when it came to uncertainties in spelling Uthman is said to 'attend to these personally'.[17] At this point, some claim that the completed Qur'an was compared with that of Aisha, another widow of the Prophet, who apparently had a Qur'an in her possession that had been dictated by the Prophet.[18] There were apparently a few errors that had to be corrected when comparing the two versions.[19] Uthman's final version was then compared against Hafsa's, who had the original version that had been completed under Abu Bakr, and that had been passed down through Umar.[20] They apparently found no differences between the version that Hafsa had and the one that Uthman had compiled.[21] Uthman then had copies made and sent to some of the major cities in the Islamic empire, probably between 4-9.[22] Uthman then ordered that all variant fragments be burned in order to have uniformity with the new official version of the Qur'an. Today orthodox Muslims believe the Qur'an at the present is Uthman's, and that it has been unaltered since that time.[23]

---

[16] Muhammad Ibn Sa'd. *Kitab al-Tabaqat al-Kubra*, ed. E. Sachau et al, 9 vols. (Leiden, 1905-1917) iii/2:62. Quoted in M. M. Al-Azami. *The History of the Qu'rānic Text: from Revelation to Compilation: A Comparative Study with the Old and New Testaments* (Leicester: UK Islamic Academy, 2003) 89.

[17] Ibn Hajar, *Fathul Bari*, ix:11, hadith no. 4987. Quoted in Al-Azami. *The History, 88.;* Al-Azami, *The History*, 90.

[18] 'Umar Ibn Shabba. *Tarikh al-Madinah al-Munawwarh*, ed. F Shaltut, 4 vols. (Jeddah, no date) 997. Quoted in M. M. Al-Azami. *The History of the Qu'rānic Text: from Revelation to Compilation: A Comparative Study with the Old and New Testaments* (Leicester: UK Islamic Academy, 2003) 91.

[19] Jalal ad-Din 'Abdur-Rahman b. Abi Bakr As-Suyuti. *al-Itqan fi 'Ulum al-Qur'an*, ed. M. Abu al-Fadl Ibrahim, 4 vols. (Cairo, 1387/1967) ii:272. Quoted in M. M. Al-Azami. *The History of the Qu'rānic Text: from Revelation to Compilation: A Comparative Study with the Old and New Testaments* (Leicester: UK Islamic Academy, 2003) 91.

[20] Al-Azami, *The History*, 93.

[21] Ibn Shabba. *Tarikh al-Madinah,* 1001-2. Quoted in Al-Azami, *The History*, 92-93.

[22] Al-Azami, *The History*, 94.

[23] Ibn Warraq, *Why I*, 74.

Criticism of the Traditional Islamic Account

Non-Muslim scholars criticize the traditional Muslim account of the Qur'an's formation. They claim that it is a patchwork of multiple stories pieced together in an attempt to fix the inconsistencies within them. Many see the traditions regarding the collection of the Qur'an as incompatible with one another. The earliest record about the compilation of the Qur'an is from 844 CE by Ibn Saad, nearly two centuries after the formation.[24] There are also no Qur'anic manuscripts attributed to Uthman that can be confidently traced to the third caliph.[25] The oldest securely dated complete Qur'an is from the 9th century.[26] Chase F. Robinson says: "Scholars committed to the idea that the history made by Muslims is comparable to that made by non-Muslims can recognize that, *taken as a whole*, the reliable evidence suggests that Qur'anic texts must have remained at least partially fluid through the late seventh and early eighth century."[27] Many Muslim scholars will disagree with these statements, and believe there is earlier evidence of the Qur'an's formation. While most Muslims believe in an earlier date for collection, the claimed date can vary from before Muhammad's death, to around 650 under Uthman.[28]

Scholars such as Michael Cook and Patricia Crone see the Muslim sources as being too late and therefore unreliable for an accurate depiction of the events surrounding the collection of

---

[24] Alphonse Mingana. "The Transmission of the Koran," in Ibn Warraq, ed. *The Origins of the Koran: Classic Essays on Islam's Holy Book* (Amherst, NY: Prometheus Books, 1998) 98.

[25] Ahmed El-Wakil. "New Light on the Collection and Authenticity of the Qur'an: The Case for the Existence of a 'Master Copy' and How It Relates to the Reading of Ḥafṣ Ibn Sulaymān from 'āṣim Ibn Abī Al-Nujūd." *Journal of Shi'a Islamic Studies* 8, no. 4 (2015): 438. https://athensstateuniversitylibrary.on.worldcat.org/oclc/6066736695.

[26] Cook, *The Koran*, 122.

[27] Chase F. Robinson. "'Abd al-Malik.Makers of the Muslim World." Oxford: Oneworld, 2005: 103. Quoted in Stephen J. Shoemaker. *Creating the Qur'an: A Historical-Critical Study* (N.p.: University of California Press, 2022) 1. https://www.amazon.com/Creating-Quran-Historical-Critical-Stephen-Shoemaker-ebook/dp/B0B13YBB27/ref=sr_1_1?crid=2OXZOIVD7JRKZ&keywords=creating+the+quran+shoemaker&qid=1694529213&s=books&sprefix=creating+the+quran+shoemaker%2Cstripbooks%2C148&sr=1-1

[28] Cook, *The Koran*, 6.

the Qur'an.[29] Cook and Crone state: 'it can be plausibly argued that the book [Koran] is the product of the belated and imperfect editing of materials from a plurality of traditions.'[30] In other words, al-Bukhari's canonical versions appear to have fused at least five earlier traditions.[31] These traditions appear to credit Abu Bakr, Umar, or Uthman individually as the sole collector of the Qur'an.[32] By combining these different contradictory traditions, al-Bukhari makes the traditional Islamic account into a seamless story that attests to the accuracy of the Qur'an. [33]

There are a few instances within the traditional account that seem to not agree with a reasonable understanding of the events. First, it is interesting that it is reported that Uthman went through an entirely new process to collect the Qur'an just for him to compare it to the one that had been compiled under Abu Bakr. Al-Azami claims this was a symbolic gesture as it would allow more people to be a part of the process.[34] The traditional account also describes the compilers openly looking for writings from anyone.[35] In some places, it describes the compilers

---

[29] Ibn Warraq, *Why I*, 81.

[30] P. Crone and M. Cook. *Hagarism: The Making of the Muslim World* (Cambridge, 1977) 18. Quoted in Ibn Warraq, *Why I Am Not A Muslim.* 2nd Ed. (N.p.: Momus and Warraq Publishers, LLC, 2020) 83.

[31] Stephen J. Shoemaker. *Creating the Qur'an: A Historical-Critical Study* (N.p.: University of California Press, 2022) Kindle, 19-20. https://www.amazon.com/Creating-Quran-Historical-Critical-Stephen-Shoemaker-ebook/dp/B0B13YBB27/ref=sr_1_1?crid=2OXZOIVD7JRKZ&keywords=creating+the+quran+shoemaker&qid=1694529213&s=books&sprefix=creating+the+quran+shoemaker%2Cstripbooks%2C148&sr=1-1.

[32] Ibid.

[33] Ibid.

[34] Al-Azami, *The History*, 93.

[35] Ibid., 82.

walking the streets asking for revelations.[36] Muslims claim that the requirement for witnesses

and other verification methods allowed only authentic revelations to make it into the final

Qur'an.

Soliciting revelations from anyone seems like an unreliable method for preserving

complete accuracy. If one's goal is to preserve the Word of God, more diligent methods would

seem more appropriate. However, some scholars argue that Abu Bakr did not want people to

claim the book only came from a select few and that is why he opened it up to such a wide

submission process from the general public.[37] The question arises: If the goal was to safeguard

the Word of God accurately, is the involvement of as many people as possible for symbolic

reasons a legitimate rationale for Uthman's duplication of the collection process? Another

questionable aspect of the traditional account is that it appears to contain inconsistencies within

itself. At one point it says that Abu Bakr required everything from written sources.[38] In other

places, it states that some of the works came from people's memories.[39]

There are also conflicting reports about whether there were differences between Abu

Bakr and Uthman's versions, as well as at what point in the process Uthman's version was

---

[36] Shauqi Daif, ed. *Kitab as-Sab'a of Ibn Mujahid* (Cairo, 1972) 6. Quoted in M. M. Al-Azami. *The History of the Qu'rānic Text: from Revelation to Compilation: A Comparative Study with the Old and New Testaments* (Leicester: UK Islamic Academy, 2003) 80

[37] Badruddin Az-Zarakhshi. *al-Burhan fi 'Ulum al-Qur'an*, ed. M. Abu al-Fadl Ibrahim, 4 vols. (Cairo, 1376/1957) i:238-239. Quoted in M. M. Al-Azami. *The History of the Qu'rānic Text: from Revelation to Compilation: A Comparative Study with the Old and New Testaments* (Leicester: UK Islamic Academy, 2003) 83.

[38] Ibn Hajar, *Fathul Bari*, ix:13. Quoted in Al-Azami. *The History,* 83.

[39] Al-Azami, *The History,* 83.; There is no consensus in Islamic sources on whether the Qur'an was transmitted by memory. See El-Wakil, "New Light," 409.

compared to Hafsa's version (as well as Aisha's).[40] Al-Azami at this point is willing to admit

that only one of the versions of Hafsa's involvement is said to have occurred. Is it a logical

argument that such a wide net was cast to collect possible revelations all for the sake of the

symbolism of allowing the participation of everyday people? Especially when one considers that

a finalized version had already been collected and preserved?

Many Muslims such as Al-Azami believe there is evidence (usually cited within the

hadiths) that the Qur'an had been written down during the life of Muhammed. Members of this

group disagree whether it had been organized into the form it is today, however, they agree that

the entirety (or at least most) of the Qur'an was written before the death of Muhammed. There

are also instances in the Qur'an that Al-Azami and others believe make it very likely that

Muhammad and his followers would have undertaken the writing and formation of the Qur'an

while he was still alive.[41] Some such as Ahmed El-Wakil believe that it is improbable that

Muhammed would not have taken steps to safeguard the Qur'an before his death.[42] The Qur'an

refers to the writing of wills, business transactions, and other documents leading to the

possibility that the Qur'an itself was also written in some form during the life of Muhammed.[43]

There appear to be a variety of different versions of Muhammad's involvement.[44] Alphonse

Mingana says:

---

[40] Al-Azami, *The History*, 88-93.

[41] Q 2:282 mentions the use of a scribe in business transactions.

[42] El-Wakil, "New Light," 411.

[43] Ibid., 426.

[44] Cook, *The Koran*, 127.

since we are not told which are the verses transmitted to Zaid by writing, and which are those that he knew only from memory, this fact cannot come, till further light dawns, into the sphere of a scientific and positive study. To believe that several verses of the Koran were written by friends of the Prophet during his lifetime is in accordance with some phrases of this sacred book which mention clearly the name of *Kitab*, 'what is written, scriptures,' but to state that the fragmentary revelations were almost entirely written and 'put promiscuously into a chest' is in contradiction to the kind of life that Muhammad led, and to early and authentic sources.[45]

It seems odd that if the book had been written during Muhammad's life, why is Zaid quoted as saying, "How can we embark on what the Prophet never did?". The question also arises, if the Qur'an had already been written down before Abu Bakr, then why would he be worried about people who had memorized the Qur'an dying in battle? Muslim scholars may refute this by saying that it was not the words of the Qur'an that were in danger of being lost, but how it was meant to be spoken or recited. It also begs the question of why there was such an effort to collect the revelations of Muhammad, as well as allow the general public's participation in the submission process, if a written version had already been compiled under the supervision of Muhammad. It seems like Al-Azami's argument for a symbolic gesture that allowed more people to feel part of the process is a poor theory if an authoritative version had come from the prophet himself.

It's also worth noting that revelations were not always revealed in order. Some verses that were revealed were added to existing suras making the idea of it being confirmed by Muhammad before his death less likely.[46] As a result, the internal composition of the Qur'an could have been altered at any time.[47] Muhammad would have had to approve the final version of the Qur'an in the last year of his life. According to Muslim traditions, this is not impossible as Muhammad was

---

[45] Mingana, "Three Ancient," 82-83.

[46] Mattson, *The Story*, 91-92.

[47] Ibid., 92.

apparently aware that his end was coming, and that the angel Gabriel reviewed the contents of the Qur'an with Muhammad.

Shoemaker comments: "It certainly is not impossible, to be sure, that much of the Qur'an had been written down before Muhammad's death. Nevertheless, I have yet to see any convincing evidence at all that could validate the claim that significant parts of the Qur'an had been written down while Muhammad was still alive."[48] There is no agreement even within Islamic sources whether the Qur'an was written down before Muhammad's death.[49]

Hadith

At this point, I will briefly diverge to talk about the hadith traditions. While the Qur'an is considered the word of God, the hadiths are the stories and sayings regarding the Prophet Muhammad. The hadiths are not considered the word of God in the same way as the Qur'an, however as most Muslims see the Prophet Muhammad as the ideal example of human behavior, his teachings are considered a great resource for understanding some of the details regarding living a proper and moral life. This work focuses on the idea of the inerrancy of the Qur'an, not the hadiths. While many Muslims may consider "authenticated" hadiths to be inerrant, that discussion is not the aim of this

. Hadiths will primarily be discussed to describe the formation of the Qur'an (where many of the accepted accounts of the Qur'an's compilation occur) and to give additional details regarding information found in the Qur'an. It is worth noting that if the Qur'an contains errors, it is unlikely that the hadith collections are inerrant.

The most widely accepted hadiths were collected two hundred years after the death of Muhammad. To verify the authenticity of a hadith, Muslims developed "Hadith Science", which is a way of gauging the validity of each hadith as well as using the narration chain associated

---

[48] Shoemaker, *Creating*, 20-21.

[49] El-Wakil, "New Light," 409.

with it. To show that the hadith can be accurately traced back to the prophet, a narration chain called the *isnad* is required. This narration chain must have only reliable and honest witnesses and the chain must be unbroken. This requirement is among other criteria that are necessary for a hadith to be considered authentic.

Much of the information regarding the formation of the Qur'anic text comes from the hadiths. Six hadith collections are considered truly authentic with al-Bukhari and Muslim's being considered the two most reliable. Bukhari died 238 years after Muhammad and over 200 years after the formation of the Qur'an.[50]

The average person may see the distortion that can occur from collecting stories nearly two centuries after their supposed occurrence. However, Muslims are confident in their Hadith Science and claim that hadiths that have been deemed authentic can be trusted as reliable sources for historical events, including those of the life of Muhammad and the formation of the Qur'an.

There is a famous study by Ignaz Goldziher that found that even hadiths that were widely accepted by the Muslim community were forgeries.[51] The theory goes that there were pious men who fabricated traditions and traced them back to the prophet.[52] This invention of hadiths may have been for political purposes.[53] Some theorize that this may have even become a type of business with there being value for those who could "acquire" hadiths that could be traced back to Muhammed.[54] Muslims widely disagree with Goldziher's findings.

Muslim scholars will point to information coming from the hadiths to argue for the historicity of the traditional Islamic account of the Qur'an. However, as can be seen above from

---

[50] Ibn Warraq, *The Origins*, 18.

[51] Ibn Warraq, *Why I*, 69

[52] Ibid., 70.

[53] Ibid.

[54] Ibid., 71.

Goldziher's study as well as other information, it is questionable whether the hadiths can be considered accurate information. Muslims admit that some hadiths are fabricated. Other hadiths contradict each other. Even some hadiths say that certain verses did not make it into Uthman's version of the Qur'an, and it is therefore incomplete.[55] Ibn Warraq sees the hadiths as useless for scientific history.[56]

There also appear to be discrepancies between Sunni and Shiite accounts of the Qur'an's formation. Al-Bukhari, "the Sunni tradition's foremost and most esteemed collector of hadith"[57], secured the traditional Islamic narrative by certifying it as "sound" in his well-known collection of hadiths.[58] However, the traditional account discussed above is significantly different to early Shiite traditions.[59]

The early Shi'i tradition of the Qur'an's composition is much different than the Sunni version that survives today.[60] Shoemaker suggests that the version of the story that Uthman collected the Qur'an was distorted in the 7th century for political purposes to reduce Ali's role in the process.[61] It is even said that Ali was named as the successor to Muhammad in the Shi'i version of the Qur'an's collection.[62] There are even Sunni narratives that describe Ali collecting

---

[55] El-Wakil, "New Light," 409.

[56] Ibn Warraq, *Why I*, 70.

[57] Shoemaker, *Creating*, 18.

[58] Ibid.

[59] Ibid.

[60] Ibid., .34.

[61] Ibid.

[62] Ibid.

the Qur'an, not Abu Bakr or Uthman.[63] Many historical sources were likely influenced by the author's Shiite or Sunni views.[64] There are records of hostility in Shi'ism to the standard Sunni text of the Qur'an.[65] Sunnis and Shiites have different positions on many first Islamic century events.[66]

Oral Traditions and Memory Research

Literacy in the early 7th century Arabia was rare, and an oral tradition likely existed during this period.[67] It is also likely that this oral tradition that the Qur'an was dependent on lasted for at least 20 years and possibly as long as a century.[68] Shoemaker summarizes the situation:

> By all indications, as we have seen, the Qur'an came into existence in a culture that was fundamentally non literate. For the first several decades of its history, its traditions circulated orally within the community, in the absence of any definitive or written version. Admittedly, it is certainly possible, if perhaps even likely, that some individuals had begun making limited notes and textual aids prior to its formal canonization. Yet the production of such rudimentary written materials does not mark a change from what was still a fundamentally oral culture in which the traditions of the Qur'an were transmitted orally... The Qur'an that we have is therefore not to be simplistically identified with what Muhammad taught his followers in Mecca and Medina, as so many modern scholars have been wont to assert. Given the conditions in which memories of his teachings circulated among his followers for decades, it is not possible that his exact words have been preserved.[69]

---

[63] Ibid.

[64] Seyfeddin Kara. "The Collection of the Qur'ān in the Early Shī'ite Discourse: The Traditions Ascribed to the Fifth Imām Abū Ja'far Muḥammad al-Bāqir." *Journal of the Royal Asiatic Society* 26, no. 3 (July 2016): 382. https://doi.org/10.1017/S1356186315000425.

[65] Cook, *The Koran*, 106.

[66] Mattson, *The Story*, 28-29.

[67] Shoemaker, *Creating*, 121.

[68] Ibid., 148.

[69] Ibid., 194.

Early on, there were very few followers of Muhammad, especially in the Meccan period, therefore, there were few people that could have been relied on for remembering the Qur'an.[70] One study suggests that the transmission of the Qur'an relied upon a semi-oral transmission and that a word-for-word dictation was not utilized.[71] If the Qur'an was primarily kept alive through oral transmission it questions the reliability of the text, especially the revelations from the early years of Islam. Shoemaker notes that while individuals may have been tasked with remembering the words of Muhammad, they would not have been able to recall his words exactly or in their entirety.[72] Human memory and oral tradition are not capable of this level of accuracy without a written tradition.[73] In other words, it would be incorrect to see these people as "human tape recorders."[74]

Oral transmission is likely to lead to a high level of omission and alteration.[75] Memory research shows that over days, even hours, there is a significant degradation in the quality and accuracy of a person's recollection.[76] While there is a widespread belief that oral cultures have an incredible capacity for accuracy compared to written cultures, studies have shown this to be false.[77] Literate societies usually have improved verbal and visual memory compared to non-

---

[70] Ibid., 126.

[71] El-Wakil, "New Light," 415.

[72] Shoemaker, *Creating*, 128.

[73] Ibid.

[74] Ibid.

[75] Ibid., 171-172.

[76] Ibid., 148-149.

[77] Ibid., 172.

literate ones.[78] Muhammad's followers would have likely been able to recall key phrases and the gist of what Muhammad taught, but not his words exactly or completely.[79] This does not mean individuals were involved in an intentional conspiracy, as many scholars theorize is the only other alternative to the traditional Islamic account.[80] Instead, these individuals were recalling the information to the best of their ability within the limitations of the human brain.[81] Fred Donner believes that large amounts of information could have been preserved and that there is a notable stability to the text of the Qur'an.[82]

The problem also arises with oral tradition where words that sound the same, but when recorded in writing may lead to different meanings in the text.[83] I explore similar variations in a later section.

Differences in Uthman's Codices

After Uthman standardized the Qur'an, he had copies made and sent to the major cities in the Islamic empire. Among these copies, it is known that there were variations within them. 36

---

[78] Ibid.

[79] Ibid., 168-169.

[80] Ibid.

[81] Ibid.

[82] Fred Donner. "The Qur'an in Recent Scholarship." in *The Quran in Its Historical Context*, ed. Gabriel Said Reynolds (London: Routledge, 2009) 42-43. Quoted in Ahmed El Wakil. "New Light on the Collection and Authenticity of the Qur'an: The Case for the Existence of a 'Master Copy' and How It Relates to the Reading of Ḥafṣ Ibn Sulaymān from ʿāṣim Ibn Abī Al-Nujūd." *Journal of Shi'a Islamic Studies* 8, no. 4 (2015): 415. https://athensstateuniversitylibrary.on.worldcat.org/oclc/6066736695

[83] Mattson, *The Story*, 96.

differences in the Qur'an sent by Uthman to the cities have been noted.[84] Scholars have argued about whether this was intentional or not. While there were different versions of non-Uthmanic codices that had completely different wordings of passages; Within the Uthmanic codex, it appears there was very little variation in the consonantal structure compared to the vowel markings.[85] These differences in the consonantal structure were usually only a single letter.[86] However, even Muslim scholars believe that the copies that Uthman had sent to the different major areas that were derived from his copy were not identical.[87] The situation is described by Sadeghi and Bergmann:

> These variants must have been introduced in Medina as the texts were copied off one another before being dispatched to the cities. They consist of small changes to the skeletal text that actually make a difference in pronunciation, usually changing one word to another (hence my label, "skeletal-morphemic" changes), as opposed to changing merely the spelling of a word. Typically, the meaning does not change. For example, in Kor 7, 75 the codex of Syria has *wa-qāla…* ('and he said') whereas others have *qāla…* ("he said"). In a few cases, the meaning is affected slightly. For example, the codex of Syria has *wa-yanšurukum…* ("makes you spread") in Kor 10, 22 whereas others have the graphically similar term *wa-yusayyirukum…* ("makes you journey").[88]

Many explanations are given among Muslim scholars for the differences in Uthman's text, some suggest that it was to accommodate multiple readings or *ahruf*. I will examine the seven readings and the seven *ahruf* below.

---

[84] Behnam Sadeghi and Uwe Bergmann. "The Codex of a Companion of the Prophet and the Qur'ān of the Prophet." *Arabica* 57, no. 4 (2010): 367. https://doi.org/10.1163/157005810X504518.

[85] Cook, *The Koran*, 119.

[86] Ibid.

[87] El-Wakil, "New Light," 418.

[88] Sadeghi and Bergmann. "The Codex," 368.

Consonants, Vowels, and Dialects

At the time the Qur'an was written down there were variables present that could lead to different readings of the text. There were variants in Qur'ans before 650 CE[89], and even some after Uthman's standardization. This includes multiple variants of the consonantal structure of the text that have been documented. This consonantal text was usually written in black. There was also no way for the vowels to be properly notated in the text, which could lead to different readings of the text, even if the consonantal structure was the same. The vowel marks were usually written in color. There were also dialectal differences that were in use as a result of slightly different versions of Arabic that were spoken by different tribes.

Compared to the consonants, the variations in vowels are more agreed upon among scholars. As Cook explains "Arabic at the time of the rise of Islam had no way of marking short vowels, and only ambiguous ways of marking long ones."[90] Ibn Mujahid (d. C.E. 935) is credited with the canonization of the system of consonants that is used today as well as placing a limit on the alternatives of vowels that are used.[91] This led to an acceptance of seven systems for vowels, however, some scholars argued that there should be even more than that.[92] Each of the seven versions was from a prominent reciter of the 8th century.[93]

---

[89] Cook, *The Koran*, 72

[90] Ibid., 67.

[91] Ibn Warraq, *Why I*, 109.

[92] Ibid.

[93] Cook, *The Koran*, 73.

These variations in vowel markings could have several effects. "For example, the word *mlk* in the fourth verse of Sura al-Fatiha can be read with a short or long vowel in the first consonant. With a short vowel the word signifies 'sovereign,' and with a long vowel the word signifies 'owner.'"[94] The vowel markings can also affect whether a verb is read in the active or passive tense.[95] "Thus a skeleton... bereft of its dots and diacritical marks, can possess several possible readings... These mean, respectively: he was killed, elephant, before, front portion of the body, to kiss and it was said."[96] Q7:163-166 is an instance where a disagreement over the correct reading has been documented. [97]

The history of the vowels could not have occurred before the Umayyad caliphate of Damascus.[98] This leads to serious questions about the preservation of Uthmanic Qur'ans before this time. Even if reciters were diligent, how can one be sure that the vowel markings that were standardized two centuries after the Qur'an was collected by Uthman are the correct reading of the text? As can be seen, there are significant differences in word choice that can occur as a result of different vowel markings.

---

[94] Mattson, *The Story*, 94.

[95] Ibid.

[96] Al-Azami, *The History*, 151.

[97] Cook, *The Koran*, 74.

[98] Mingana, "Three Ancient," 91.

Some claim that Mujahid was not trying to finalize the canon, including the vowels.[99] This would have been a lost cause by the 4th/10th century,[100] and the claims of exclusivity would come later.[101] Mujahid was just trying to "bring order and clarity", he never claimed comprehensiveness.[102] As Intisar A. Rabb puts it: "Ibn Mujāhid sought not to limit and exclude all but his list of seven readings; he aimed to announce and apply criteria for distinguishing acceptable from truly unacceptable ratings, in response to the increase in potentially questionable readings."[103]

Therefore, "the boundary between acceptable and unacceptable readings remained somewhat blurred."[104] As the Encylopaedia of the Quran says: "Not much can be said with certainty about the actual occurrence of the different readings, or whether most of them had anything more than theoretical significance. The analysis of the numerous preserved historical Qur'an manuscripts should be of great help in establishing a clearer picture, but these data have only begun to be analyzed".[105]

---

[99] Intisar A. Rabb and انتصار رب. "Non-Canonical Readings of the Qur'an: Recognition and Authenticity (the Ḥimṣī Reading) / قراءة حمص: قراءة غير متواترة." *Journal of Qur'anic Studies* 8, no. 2 (2006): 105. https://athensstateuniversitylibrary.on.worldcat.org/oclc/9972065557

[100] Ibid.

[101] Ibid., 106.

[102] Ibid., 105-106.

[103] Ibid., 109.

[104] Frederik Leemhuis. "Readings of the Qur'ān." In *Encyclopaedia of the Qur'ān*, edited by Jane Dammen McAuliffe. Leiden: Brill, 2004. 359. https://archive.org/details/encyclopaedia-of-the-quran-6-volumes-jane-dammen-mc-auliffe/page/n2213/mode/2up.

[105] Ibid., 360.

Mujahid was criticized for his decision to choose seven readings as many believed this would make people confuse the seven readings with the seven *ahruf* which I will discuss below.[106] While some scholars equate the seven readings with the seven *ahruf*, many see them as independent traditions.

The Seven Ahruf

Some traditions attest that Muhammad believed the Qu'ran was revealed in seven forms known as the seven *ahruf*. One story tells of a dispute where two people who both had heard their version from Muhammad, argued over the correct reading. The story goes:

> It is narrated from 'Umar Ibn al Khaṭṭāb [that] he said: 'I heard Hishām Ibn Hakīm reciting *Sūrat al Furqān* during the lifetime of Allah's Messenger. I listened to his recitation and noticed that he recited in several different ways which Allah's Messenger had not taught me. I was about to jump on him during his prayer but I controlled my temper. When he had completed his prayer, I put his upper garment around his neck and seized him by it and said, 'Who taught you this surah which I heard you reciting?' He said, 'Allah's Messenger taught it to me.' I said, 'You have told a lie, for Allah's Messenger has taught it to me in a way different from yours.' So I dragged him to Allah's Messenger and said (to Allāh's Messenger), 'I heard this person reciting *Sūrat al Furqān* in a way which you have not taught me.' On that, Allah's Messenger said, 'Release him (O 'Umar)! Recite O Hishām!' Then he recited in the same way as I heard him reciting. Then Allah's Messenger said, 'It was revealed in this way' and added 'Recite O 'Umar.' I recited it as he had taught me. Allah's Messenger then said, 'It was revealed in this way. This Qur'an has been revealed to be recited in seven *ahruf*, so recite of it whichever is easier for you.'[107]

As can be seen, Muhammad is believed to have approved of both of their different versions. Muslim scholars argue that these differences in versions do not affect the interpretation

---

[106] Rabb and انتصار رب. "Non-Canonical Readings," 104.

[107] Abu 'Abd Allah Muhammad Ibn Ismail Al Bukhari. *Al Jami' al Sahih* or *Sahih al Bukhari*. 9 vols. With English translation by Muhammad Muhsin Khan. 2nd ed. (Ankara: n.d) 6:481-482. Quoted in Ahmad 'Alī Al Imām. *Variant Readings of the Qur'an: A Critical Study of Their Historical and Linguistic Origins* (Beltsville, MD: International Graphics, 1998) 3-4. https://archive.org/details/VARIANTREADINGSOFTHEQURANACRITICALSTUDYOFTHEIRHISTORICALANDLINGUISTICORIGINS.

of the text. Many see them as similar to the differences among versions of English such as the spelling of "color" vs "colour".

There seems to be a lack of consensus on exactly what the term *ahruf* (singular: *harf*) means, especially as described in early Islamic history. At different points in history, the term *harf* has indicated a manner of pronunciation, variant reading, as well as seemingly other meanings.[108] The variants described encompass a variety of areas including different verbal forms, synonyms, and interpolations of entire phrases.[109]

Many believe that the *ahruf* describes seven different dialects that were used by some of Muhammad's early followers.[110] El-Wakil appears to take this position: "Different interpretations have been given as to what the seven a*hruf* constitute, though the most reasonable opinion appears to be that they reflected the different dialects of the various Arabian tribes."[111] However, this argument does not remedy the belief that Umar and Hisham were both of the Quarashi tribe, and therefore it would have been unlikely that they reported different dialectical

---

[108] Leemhuis, "Readings," 354.

[109] Ibid.

[110] Theodor Nöldeke. "The Koran," in Ibn Warraq, ed. *The Origins of the Koran: Classic Essays on Islam's Holy Book* (Amherst, NY: Prometheus Books, 1998) 40.

[111] El-Wakil, "New Light," 412.

readings of the Qur'an.[112] There are different dialects identified in the Qur'an suggesting that

Uthman's version is not just as simple as referring to the Quarashi dialect.[113]

As can be seen, not everyone agrees exactly what is meant by *ahruf*. Al-Imam, a Muslim

scholar, in his book *Variant Readings of the Qur'an: A Critical Study of Their Historical and

Linguistic Origins* sums up the main theories on what exactly is a *harf*:

1. "They are ambiguous and their meaning cannot be known with certainty because the word *harf* has different meanings: a letter of the alphabet, a word, a meaning, or a way."[114]

2. "The word *harf* may mean 'ways of pronunciation,' which was the view of al Khalīl Ibn Ahmad (170/786)."[115]

3. "The seven a*hruf* indicate seven meanings."[116]

4. "The seven a*hruf* are ways of recitation using synonyms, for example, *ta'āl, aqbil, 'ajjil, asri'*."[117]

5. "The seven a*hruf* are seven dialects of the Arabs."[118]

6. "The seven a*hruf* indicate seven varieties and differences in the readings."[119]

---

[112] Ahmad 'Alī Al Imām. *Variant Readings of the Qur'an: A Critical Study of Their Historical and Linguistic Origins* (Beltsville, MD: International Graphics, 1998) 103. https://archive.org/details/VARIANTREADINGSOFTHEQURANACRITICALSTUDYOFTHEIRHISTORICALA NDLINGUISTICORIGINS.

[113] Ibid.

[114] Ibid., 10.

[115] Ibid.

[116] Ibid., 11.

[117] Ibid., 12.

[118] Ibid., 13.

[119] Ibid., 15.

7.   "A difference in letters or augment (e.g., *wa mā 'amilathu/wa mā 'amilat)?*"[120]

Al-Imam summarizes: "Finally, although scholars disagree as to the meaning of the *aḥruf*, the most natural interpretation is that they refer to linguistic variations in the manner of reciting the Qur'an. However, it is difficult to commit to any of the specific definitions of these linguistic variations advanced by various scholars."[121] There is also a debate about whether the number seven is meant to be exact. Most scholars say that the number seven represents exactly seven, however, there is a small group that believes that seven is not exact, but still believe that the *aḥruf* number less than 10.[122]

The concept of the seven *aḥruf* has been used to explain the differences in the codices sent to the different cities after Uthman's standardization. Some say it is only a single *harf*. Al-Imam's conclusion:

> As to the relation between the 'Uthmānic *maṣāḥif* and the seven *aḥruf*, the most acceptable two opinions among the scholars are that the 'Uthmānic *maṣāḥif* accommodate either all or some of the *aḥruf*, which correspond with the orthography of the 'Uthmānic *maṣāḥif* (including what is transmitted by *tawātur* but not *āḥād* readings attributed to certain personal codices and transmitted to us in unauthentic chains). The *maṣāḥif* were recorded in one *harf* with the permission to recite in seven *aḥruf*.[123]

Al-Imam further explains: "Finally, the *maṣāḥif* are said to contain as much of the *aḥruf* as can be accommodated within the orthography of the Qur'an, according to the final revealed

---

[120] Ibid., 16.

[121] Ibid., 20.

[122] Ibid., 7.

[123] Ibid., 172.

version—the view attributed to most scholars. Conse-quently, the *maṣāḥif* include an undefined number of a*ḥruf* certainly more than one *ḥarf* but not all seven a*ḥruf*."[124]

There is also the question if synonyms can be used within different versions of the Qur'an, and there are many different views on the topic. The inclusion of synonyms leads to massive questions regarding the inerrancy of the Qur'an. An example of a different word possibly being allowed by Allah and the Prophet Muhammed is the difference in Sura al-Fatiha in the fourth verse where both the words *mālik* (owner) and *malik* (king) are allowed (this example can also be seen when discussing the seven readings where "sovereign" and "owner" were used).[125] Al-Imam believes it is unacceptable to use synonyms as Allah has chosen a precise word for a reason.[126]

Summary

At times the traditional Islamic account of the collection of the Qur'an seems to have numerous faults. This account appears to collect and combine a variety of different stories on the Qur'an's collection, many of which do not seem to be able to coexist. There are an assortment of issues, such as the unnecessary aspect of recompiling the Qur'an under Uthman if it had already been collected under Abu Bakr, and even possibly Muhammed himself. Also, the collection of Qur'anic fragments from the general population does not inspire confidence when considering the Qur'an is claimed to have no errors, and the argument that this was done for symbolic reasons seems lacking. There are also other questions in this account including Zaid's hesitation

---

[124] Ibid., 66.

[125] Al-Azami, *The History*, 155.

[126] Al Imām, *Variant Readings*, xviii.

to do something that Muhammad had not done himself, collect the Qur'an; something that Abu

Bakr may have said as well. Also, there may be conflicting reports on Hafsa's and Aisha's roles

in the process.

Even if the Qur'an was collected with complete accuracy under Uthman or another

before him, there seem to be issues even after this point. Even Muslim scholars such as Al-

Azami admit that there were differences in the first Qur'ans copied from Uthman's codex that

were sent to the major cities of the Islamic empire. Not only are there differences in the

consonantal structure of the Qur'ans distributed by Uthman, but there is even more variance

among other Qur'ans that have been dated after Uthman's collection. Even if for the sake of

argument one accepts that the consonantal structure only had dialectal differences or minor

errors, there is still the question of the accuracy of the Qur'an given the lack of vowel markings.

These markings can create completely different words, and these vowels were not standardized

till about 250 years later. Even if reciters were sent along to ensure correct readings, it seems

very unlikely that no variances would have arisen as time went on and as the Qur'an

disseminated further and further into distant lands. Muslims will claim that it would be

impossible for variants to occur because any variant that did arise would immediately be

corrected by the majority of other Qur'ans that had been accurately preserved. This seems to be

an optimistic view in an oral society that would have had few written versions of the Qur'an and

a highly illiterate population. This is especially important if one considers the fallibility of oral

tradition and human memory.

As can be seen, many of the accounts of the Qur'an's formation have come from the

hadiths which were not standardized until the 9th century, over 200 years after the events. Other accounts come from the biographies of Muhammad which are considered, even by Muslims, to be even less reliable. The collection of these hadiths and the accuracy that they claim, even if one considers Hadith Science, is dubious. Also, some hadith collections seem to come into conflict not only with other hadiths but possibly with themselves. Welch comments on the Abu Bakr account: "there are serious problems with this account, …most of the key points in this story are contradicted by alternative accounts in the canonical hadith collections and other early Muslim sources."[127] Even after Uthman there appeared to be different versions of the Qur'anic text that existed. These are found not only on coins but also on the inscriptions on the Dome of the Rock.

Muslim scholars such as Al-Azami use terms like "highest attainable accuracy"[128] and "as sincere an effort as possible"[129] when describing the formation of the Qur'an. It does seem evident that there was diligence done in collecting the Qur'an, especially compared to other religious scriptures. However, "highest attainable accuracy" and "sincere effort" do not mean inerrancy.

For the Qur'an to be completely without error, one must believe several things. First, the Qur'an was accurately remembered and recalled by the people of Muhammad's time. Second, all this information was collected in its entirety with no additions or omissions. Third, the apparent inconsistencies within the traditional Islamic account are not actually in conflict with each other.

---

[127] A.T. Welch. "al-Kur'an," In *El²* 5:400-429 (Leidin: Brill, 1986) 404-405. Quoted in Stephen J. Shoemaker. *Creating the Qur'an: A Historical-Critical Study* (N.p.: University of California Press, 2022) 23. https://www.amazon.com/Creating-Quran-Historical-Critical-Stephen-Shoemaker-ebook/dp/B0B13YBB27/ref=sr_1_1?crid=2OXZOIVD7JRKZ&keywords=creating+the+quran+shoemaker&qid=1694529213&s=books&sprefix=creating+the+quran+shoemaker%2Cstripbooks%2C148&sr=1-1

[128] Al-Azami, *The History*, 82.

[129] Ibid., 86.

Fourth, the reciters were able to perfectly preserve the Qur'an despite consonantal and vowel issues. Fifth, the hadiths and biographies that recall this information have been accurately recorded. Sixth, the explanation of the seven readings and seven *ahruf* are legitimate explanations for variations. This is just to name some of the variables that had to go exactly right for the Qur'an that is used today to be inerrant.

CHAPTER TWO

A BRIEF HISTORY OF ISLAMIC VIEWS ON QUR'ANIC INERRANCY

Did most Muslims always believe in inerrancy? Was this a belief that was consistently held from the time of the Prophet until now? While the specific views that Islamic groups and individuals held on inerrancy are hard to determine definitively, some are considered to have questioned aspects of the Qur'an.

Views of Notable Islamic Groups

After the death of Muhammad and the reign of the first caliphs, the Umayyads reigned from 661 to 750 CE.[1] Around this time a group arose called the Kharijites, who were often considered puritans and extremists.[2] Before their beliefs became fixed they showed rationalist tendencies.[3] One group among them even doubted the reliability of the Qur'an, and some questioned whether the story of Joseph should be included in the Qur'an.[4] Another group known as the Qadarites are known to have upheld the notion of free will.[5] Goldziher believes this was an

---

[1] Ibn Warraq, *Why I*, 242-243.

[2] Ibid., 243.

[3] Ibid., 244.

[4] Ibid.

[5] Ibid., 244.

important first step away from the dominance of traditional notions.[6] The views of the Qadarites

undermined Islamic orthodoxy.[7]

There is probably no other major Islamic group known for their rationalism than the

Mutazilites. They were known to have questioned the reliability of the Qur'an.[8] Steiner calls

them the "freethinkers of Islam" however there is no sign that they had absolute liberated

thinking.[9] They are also known for introducing Greek philosophical ideas as well as their

skepticism.[10]

The Mutazilites doubted the inimitability of the Qur'an which is considered the main test

of authenticity given within the Qur'an itself, believing that there was nothing miraculous about

the book's style and composition.[11] The Mutazilites believe that humans were capable of

imitating the Qur'an, but God stops them.[12] They take a more allegorical approach as in the case

of considering the anthropomorphisms of God in the Qur'an.[13] They also questioned the

authenticity of certain verses where the prophet utters curses, as well as, questioned the

---

[6] Ignaz Goldziher. *Introduction to Islamic Theology and Law*. Translated by Andras and Ruth Hamori (Princeton, 1981) 82. Quoted in Ibn Warraq, *Why I Am Not A Muslim*. 2nd Ed. (N.p.: Momus and Warraq Publishers, LLC, 2020) 245.

[7] Ibn Warraq, *Why I*, 245.

[8] Ibid., 247.

[9] Ibn Warraw, *Why I*, 245.

[10] Ibid.

[11] Ibid., 247.

[12] Ulrika Mårtensson. "Al-Ṭabarī's Concept of the Qur'an: A Systemic Analysis." *Journal of Qur'anic Studies* = Magallat Ad-Dirasat Al-Quraniya 18, no. 2 (2016): 24-25. https://doi.org/10.3366/jqs.2016.0238.

[13] Ibn Warraq, *Why I*, 246.

authenticity of many hadiths.[14] However, the traditionalist view ultimately prevailed and al-Ashari is seen to have given the death blow to Mutazilism.[15]

The Abbasids deposed the Umayyads and were considered a fundamentalist group.[16] Under the Abbasids there were two inquisitions and upon their end Caliph Mutawakkil declared the Mutazilite doctrines heretical and went back to the traditional faith.[17] As Nicholson puts it: "henceforth there was a little room in Islam for independent thought. The populace regarded philosophy and natural science as a species of infidelity. Authors of works on these subjects ran a serious risk unless they disguised their true opinions and brought the results of their investigations into apparent conformity with the text of the Koran."[18] Ibn Mujahid who is credited with the seven readings, was supported by the Abbasid authorities.[19]

Other groups also questioned traditional Islamic views such as the Sufis, who believed that true religion had nothing to do with doctrinal and the legal system of orthodoxy.[20] The text of the Qur'an was further steadied in the tenth/sixteenth century with the help of the Ottoman Empire.[21] The Ottoman Empire implemented the Hafs 'an 'Asim reading, and this reading was

---

[14] Ibid., 247-248.

[15] Ibid., 249-250.

[16] Ibid., 242.

[17] Ibid., 280.

[18] R.A. Nicholson. *Literary History of the Arabs* (Cambridge, 1930) 284. Quoted in Ibn Warraq, *Why I Am Not A Muslim*. 2nd Ed. (N.p.: Momus and Warraq Publishers, LLC, 2020) 280.

[19] Leemhuis, "Readings," 357.

[20] Ibn Warraq, *Why I*, 276.

[21] Leemhuis, "Readings," 361.

further standardized with the Egyptian government's edition of the Qur'an in 1342/1923.[22]

Outside of this reading, only the Nafi' reading is utilized, albeit to a substantially lesser degree.[23]

While major Islamic groups had significant influence during their respective eras, the situation

varied "from country to country, ruler to ruler, period to period."[24]

Variant Texts

Many variant versions of the Qur'an have survived throughout Islamic history. Even after

Uthman's standardization and the subsequent burning of variant texts, many of these variants

have survived as is evident from manuscripts and other Islamic literature. As Charles Adams

said, "literally thousands of variant readings of particular verses were known in the first three

(Muslim) centuries."[25] In other words, Uthman did not completely eliminate differences but

reduced them.[26]

There is evidence that contemporaries and successors of Muhammad had their own

collections which differed from Muhammad's.[27] "Manuscript evidence now corroborates pre-

modern reports about the existence of Companion codices, their having different *sūra* orderings,

---

[22] Ibid.

[23] Ibid.

[24] Ibn Warraq, *Why I*, 280.

[25] C. J. Adams. "Quran: The Text and Its History," in *Encyclopedia of Religion*, Mircea Eliade, editor-in-chief (New York, London. Macmillan, 1987) 157-176. Quoted in Ibn Warraq, ed. *The Origins of the Koran: Classic Essays on Islam's Holy Book* (Amherst, NY: Prometheus Books, 1998) 15.

[26] Rabb and انتصار رب. "Non-Canonical Readings," 100.

[27] Ibid., 86.

and, to an extent, the nature of their verbal differences."[28] Companions with personal codices

include ibn Masud, ibn Ka'b, al-Ash'ari, ibn Abbas, and ibn Malik.[29]

There are variant texts that have been dated to after Uthman's standardization. Some of

these variants are more prominent than one might expect. Shoemaker elaborates:

> The degree to which the Qur'an remained an unstable text in Islamic usage during the
> first few centuries of Islam remains effectively still unknown in the absence of concerted
> study of these variants and their relation to the invariable, now canonical, text. Yet their
> mere existence raises questions about the state of the Qur'an well beyond al-Ḥajjāj and
> 'Abd al-Malik. So, too, do the Qur'anic inscriptions of the Dome of the Rock that were
> installed by 'Abd al-Malik. These inscriptions are our earliest surviving evidence for the
> text of the Qur'an, and yet they differ from the now canonical version of the Qur'an. How
> can this be, especially if the text of the Qur'an had already been firmly established
> already for forty years since the reign of Uthmān? It would appear that even at the close
> of the seventh century, as al-Ḥajjāj's efforts were presumably about to get underway, the
> official version of the Qur'an, in Jerusalem at least, was different from the received
> text.[30]

Michael Cook adds "Equally, when the first Koranic quotations appear on coins and

inscriptions towards the end of the seventh century, they show divergences from the canonical

text. These are trivial from the point of view of content, but the fact that they appear in such

formal context as these goes badly with the notion that the text had already been frozen."[31]

---

[28] Sadeghi and Bergmann, "The Codex," 412.

[29] Mustafa Shah. "The Case of Variae Lectiones in Classical Islamic Jurisprudence: Grammar and the Interpretation of Law." *International Journal for the Semiotics of Law - Revue Internationale De Sémiotique Juridique* 29, no. 2 (2016): 285–311. https://doi.org/10.1007/s11196-016-9461-1.

[30] Shoemaker, *Creating*, 63-64.

[31] M. Cook. *Muhammad* (Oxford: 1983) 65. Quoted in Ibn Warraq, ed. *The Origins of the Koran: Classic Essays on Islam's Holy Book* (Amherst, NY: Prometheus Books, 1998) 27.

After the standardization by Uthman, these texts may not have been as taboo as it appears. Many prominent scholars passed down non-Uthmanic versions.[32] Variant readings may have been used as tools in areas such as legal discourse, however, they likely would have been considered subordinate to the canonical text.[33] Al-Mardāwī (d. 885/1480) believed that reciting *shādhdha*[34] in worship should be discouraged.[35]

It seems that as time went on variant texts were seen as less acceptable. There are famous stories of individuals such as Ibn Shunbundh and Ibn Miqsam being prosecuted because of variant texts. Under the chairmanship of Ibn Mujahid, Ibn Shunbundh was sentenced to be beaten and was forbidden from reading variant texts.[36] Similarly, Ibn Miqsam was forced to renounce his belief that he was able to determine for himself the proper punctuation and vocalization of the text.[37]

---

[32] Sadeghi and Bergmann, "The Codex," 371.

[33] Shah, "The Case," 285-311.

[34] "*shādhdh* is a reading that has been narrated as Qur'an without a successive transmission or at least a famous (*mashhūr*) transmission accepted by the people." See Al Imam, *Variant Readings*, 131.

[35] Shah, "The Case," 285-311.

[36] Al Imam, *Variant Readings*, 124.

[37] R. Paret. "Kirā'a." In *The Encyclopaedia of the Islam*, edited by C. E. Bosworth, E. Van Donzel, B. Lewis and Ch. Pellat (Leiden: E.J. Brill, 1986) 127. https://archive.org/details/ei2-complete/Encyclopaedia_of_Islam_vol_5_1/page/126/mode/2up.

There are thousands of textual variants of the Qur'an that are known to have survived.[38]

Many manuscript differences are due to scribal errors[39], and the largest category of variations is often attributed to being similar to the earlier example of the use of "color" versus "colour" in different versions of English.[40] However, the situation may be more complicated than this. Even Islamic tradition appears to admit that Qur'an 3:144 is a later addition.[41] Sources say that certain experts during these early times disagreed on what constituted the authoritative Qur'an.[42] Two examples of verses that were not included in the Qur'an but may have been originally supposed to be are the Verse of the Stoning and Valleys of Gold:

> Ubai b. Ka'b said to me, 'O Zirr, how many verses did you count (or how many verses did you read) in Surat al-Ahzab?' 'Seventy-two or seventy-three,' I answered. Said he, 'Yet it used to be equal to Surat al-Baqara (ii), and we used to read in it the Verse of Stoning.' Said I, 'And what is the Verse of Stoning?' He said, 'If a grown man and woman commit adultery, stone them without hesitation, as a warning from Allah, for Allah is mighty, wise.'
> There was revealed a sura about the size of al-Bara'a (ix), which was later withdrawn, of which I remember (the words) 'Allah will help along this religion by means of a people for whom is no portion. Had the son of Adam two valleys full of gold he would yearn for a third. Nothing will really fill man's belly but the dust, and Allah turns to whom He will.'[43]

---

[38] Shoemaker, *Creating*, 208.

[39] Daniel A. Brubaker. *Corrections in Early Qur'ān Manuscripts: Twenty Examples* (Lovettsville, VA: Think and Tell Press, 2019) 95. https://archive.org/details/corrections-in-early-quran-manuscripts-daniel-a-brubaker/mode/2up.

[40] Sadeghi and Bergmann, "The Codex," 373.

[41] Shoemaker, *Creating*, 221.

[42] El-Wakil, "New Light," 410.

[43] Jeffery, "Abu 'Ubaid," 151-152.

Sometimes abrogation is used as a reason for why certain verses no longer exist, as once they were abrogated they no longer were to be included in the Qur'an.[44] However, this is not always the case as some abrogated verses are still included in the Qur'an. Abrogation will be discussed further in Chapter Three.

There is much about the history of divergent traditions that is still not known.[45] It appears there were numerous in the early centuries, however, today there is only one single dominant tradition.[46] While the majority of the differences in Qur'anic texts were minor, there are variants whose changes had a more significant impact.

Ibn Masud and Ubayy Ka'b

There are probably no more famous stories of variant texts than those of Ibn Masud and Ubayy Ka'b. This is because these two men were considered reliable authorities on the Qur'an, with Masud even being one of the four people that Muhammed personally endorsed as someone the community could turn to for instruction on the Qur'an.[47] Umar also attested to Masud's competence.[48]

Ibn Masud's variant is said to have differed from Uthman's on 102 instances,[49] and is believed to have rejected the Fatihah inclusion, and the words of suras 113 and 114.[50] Even the

---

[44] El-Wakil, "New Light," 412-413.

[45] Cook, *The Koran*, 74.

[46] Ibid.

[47] Jeffery, "Materials," 127.

[48] Al-Azami, *The History*, 85.

[49] Al Imam, *Variant Readings*, 86.

[50] Ibn Warraq, *Why I*, 106.

widow of Muhammad, Aisha, is storied to have quoted Ibn Masud's version.[51] There are different views of what Ibn Masud's variant represented, whether this was a rejection of the Uthmanic codex, or whether Ibn Masud kept the variants as a resource, but acknowledged they were inferior to Uthman's version.[52] Muslim scholars have different views on Ibn Masud, and his variant is often discussed in works that deal with the formation of the Qur'an. Some accept the story of Ibn Masud's defiance, while most appear to either deny it or have other explanations for his variant texts. Ibn Masud is thought to have felt overlooked or insulted when he was not asked to join the committee in charge of compiling the Qur'an.[53] He is quoted as remarking that he had already been taught by the Prophet while Zaid was still a child.[54] It is said that Ibn Masud refused to give back his Qur'an when Uthman was burning variant texts and instructed his students to do likewise.[55]

It seems that Ibn Masud's codex and other variant texts were still openly discussed in the second Islamic century.[56] An example of a difference between Uthman's and Ibn Masud's texts can be seen in the following passages of Q 44:54: 'and we shall support them with grayish white ones, with beautiful eyes' instead of 'and we shall pair them off with white ones, with beautiful eyes'.[57] It seems that Ibn Masud's version was still used as a resource even though many scholars did not see it as canonical. "In connection with Q 17:93, 'Abd al-Razzāq mentions a tradition from Mujāhid: 'We did not know what 'a house of ornament (*zukhruf*)' was until we

---

[51] Shah, "The Case," 285-311.

[52] Al Imam, *Variant Readings*, 172.

[53] Ibid., 29.

[54] Ibid.

[55] Ibid.

[56] Leemhuis, "Readings," 354.

[57] Ibid.

saw in the *qirā'a* of Ibn Mas'ūd 'a house of gold (*dhahab*).'"[58] Ubayy Ka'b (d. either 26/649 or 34/654[59]) is another famous example of a variant text. Ka'b believed that some suras had verses removed, and also included two suras not in Uthman's codex.[60]

Ultimately most Muslim scholars see the presence of the Ibn Masud's and Ka'b's variants as either unauthentic or that they were merely references, not to be seen as equal to Uthman's codex. Al-Imam concludes: "The additional interpolations attributed to the personal codices are found to be their own explanations and interpretations. They all are generally isolated reports (*akhbār āḥād*), dubious, or rejected."[61] Al-Imam continues: "The accounts alleging that Ubayy added to his *muṣhaf* the *du'ā' al qunūt* as one or two surahs and that Ibn Mas'ūd denied *al Fātiḥah* and *al Mu'awwidhatayn* are to be regarded as unauthentic."[62]

It is interesting that people who are considered so reliable on the Qur'an and to have been endorsed by Muhammad, appear to sanction variant texts other than Uthman. While the interpretation of these accounts are debatable, if Ibn Masud and Ka'b rejected the Uthmanic codex then it leads to serious questions on the reliability of the canonical text.

Other Notable Individuals

Other individuals commented on the inerrancy of the Qur'an. One of the first of these is a scribe who noticed that Muhammad was less strict with how the Qur'an was recorded than later Muslims would believe. It is storied that some of Muhammad's scribes would alter the text of the

---

[58] Ibid.

[59] Paret, "Kirā'a," 127.

[60] El-Wakil, "New Light," 413.

[61] Al Imam, *Variant Readings*, 172.

[62] Ibid.

Qur'an.[63] Muhammad is said to have not objected to these changes.[64] As a result, the scribe is said to have left Islam and returned to Mecca.[65] This story's authenticity is questioned by many Muslim scholars. However, other detractors' accounts are much clearer.

Dja'd b. Dirham (executed in 105/723) is usually named as Islam's first detractor.[66] Other notable early Muslims such as Muhammad's widow, Aisha, are reported to have questioned the now standardized text. Aisha is reported to have said: "During the times of the Prophet, the chapter of the Parties used to be two hundred verses when read. When 'Uthman edited the copies of the Koran, only the current (versus) were recorded".[67]

One area where the Qur'an was repeatedly challenged was the claim that the text could not be imitated. Many individuals commented on or attempted to disprove the theory of inimitability.[68] These individuals include Bashshār b. Burd (d. 166/783), Abu'l-'Atāhiya (d. 213/828), Abū Mūsā 'Isā b. Sabīh, and Ibn al-Rāwandi (d. 250/864, 297/910, or 299/912).[69]

---

[63] Ibid., 60.

[64] Ibid.

[65] Ibid.

[66] G. E. Von Grunebaum. "I'djāz." In *The Encyclopaedia of the Islam*, edited by B. Lewis, V. L. Menage, Ch. Pellat and + J. Schacht (Leiden: E.J. Brill, 1986) 1019. https://archive.org/details/ei2-complete/Encyclopaedia_of_Islam_vol_3_H-Iram/page/1018/mode/2up.

[67] Ibn Warraq, *The Origins*, 14.

[68] Von Grunebaum, "I'djāz," 1019.

[69] Ibid.

Al-Razi, who lived 865-925 CE, is perhaps the greatest freethinker in Islam.[70] He believed the Qur'an was not inimitable and saw the texts as being a long way from flawless.[71] He also denied creation ex nihlio or the idea that the earth was created out of nothing.[72] He may have had the most violent criticism of religion in the Middle Ages, whether by a European or Muslim.[73]

Some appear to support the inerrancy of the Qur'an. Al-Tabari was sympathetic to the traditionalist camp's view and often was against the rationalist doctrine, especially in terms of the created Qur'an.[74] At other times it seems that Al-Tabari made a distinction between the Qur'an that was sent down from God and the written text.[75] He believed they could be the same, but they also might not be.[76] Scholars theorize that Al-Tabari believed the Qur'an was uncreated and inimitable.[77] Al-Tabari includes the infamous story of the Satanic Verses, an instance where Muhammad was apparently tricked by Satan into believing Allah had sent a revelation that allowed for polytheism.[78] Muslim scholars such as Al-Azami reject the story of the Satanic

---

[70] Ibn Warraq, *Why I*, 266.

[71] Ibid., 268.

[72] Ibid., 267.

[73] Ibid., 269.

[74] Mårtensson, "Al-Ṭabarī's," 9.

[75] Ibid., 29.

[76] Ibid., 29.

[77] Ibid., 43.

[78] Ibn Warraq, *Why I*, 102.

Verses and believe that Al-Tabari included these only for "curiosity value".[79] Al-Tabari also believed that Uthman's text was only one *harf*.[80]

Another apparent supporter of Qur'anic inerrancy was Ibn al Baqillani, who believed the entire Qur'an was contained in Uthman's codex, excluding the abrogated verses.[81] He believed that it was in the same arrangement and that the contents were what was revealed to the Prophet and that there was no difference in word order.[82] Likewise, Ibn Hazm believed that every letter was in the same position as it was when revealed to Muhammed.[83]

Al-Ghazali, who is sometimes referred to as the greatest Muslim after Muhammed, is seen to have ended Islam's "love affair with Greek philosophy and rationalism".[84] His condemnation of philosophical speculation is considered a "turning point in the intellectual history of Islam".[85] Al-Ghazali led Muslims back to an unquestioning faith in the Qur'an, and for it to be accepted literally.[86] At this point, the gains of the rationalist Mutazilites were wasted.[87]

---

[79] Al-Azami, *The History*, 309-310.

[80] Al Imam, *Variant Readings*, 65-66.

[81] Ibid., 39.

[82] Ibid.

[83] Al Imam, *Variant Readings*, 39-40. The view that every letter is in the correct place does not seem to be able to coexist with the "color" vs "colour" argument.

[84] Ibn Warraq, *Why I*, 264.

[85] Ibid.

[86] Ibid., 265.

[87] Ibid.

Muslim views on Qur'anic inerrancy are not always easy to nail down. It seems that fairly early on in Islamic history the belief that the Qur'an contained no errors and had been preserved perfectly, is apparent for the majority of Muslim scholars. As the Encylopaedia of Islam puts it: "Muslim tradition identifies a comparatively small number of outspoken critics of the Book."[88] However, there are outliers from this theory. Early Muslim scholars appear to have been much more flexible than modern:[89]

> While modern Muslims may be committed to an impossibly conservative position, Muslim scholars of the early years of Islam were far more flexible in their position, realizing that parts of the Koran were lost, perverted, and that there were many thousand variants which made it impossible to talk of *the* Koran. For example, as-Suyuti (died 1505), one of the most famous and revered of the commentators of the Koran, quotes Ibn 'Umar al-khattab as saying: 'Let none of you say that he has acquired the entire Koran for how does he know that it is all? Much of the Koran has been lost, thus to let him say, 'I have acquired of it what is available'.[90]

It is possible that due to the lack of reliable sources from the first two centuries of Islam modern audiences may not fully realize the different opinions on Qur'anic inerrancy. However, by the time of Ibn Mujahid and others of the late second to early third Islamic century, the theory of Qur'anic inerrancy seems to be very widespread. At this point going against this belief could bring about serious consequences such as discreditation or even legal and physical punishment. As with many details of the first 200 years of Islamic history, one is often at the mercy of Muslim scholars who are not always unbiased in their accounts and are often optimistic about the early history as it pertains to verifying their contemporary Muslim beliefs. Modern audiences are often solely reliant upon sources such as the sira and hadiths, which are questionable especially outside of Muslim discourse.

---

[88] Von Grunebaum, "I'djāz," 1019.

[89] Ibn Warraq, *The Origins*, 14.

[90] Ibid.

CHAPTER THREE

EXAMINATION OF QUR'ANIC INERRANCY

Is there a way to determine if the claim of Qur'anic inerrancy is legitimate? Are there demonstratable errors within the text that cannot be reconciled by allegory or some other explanation? Q 4:82 says: "Then do they not reflect upon the Qur'ān? If it had been from [any] other than Allāh, they would have found within it much contradiction."[1] I will take a look at some examples that may provide a better understanding of the theory of Qur'anic inerrancy.

Historicity

The historicity of a text is a great way to determine if the information that is given matches what is known from other sources. Of course, this is often based on archaeological data or other methods of determining history, which leads to questions of the authenticity or interpretation of this data. Also, not everything within the Qur'an may have been intended to be a historical account. For example, there are often stories within religious texts that are meant to be parables or something similar. It is not always easy to determine what is meant to be taken historically and what is meant to be taken figuratively. Yet, sometimes it can be fairly obvious to determine what was meant to be historical.

Muhammad

References to Muhammad are occasional and brief in non-Islamic sources.[2] Secular references exist but provide little detail.[3] The earliest extant biography of Muhammad's life is

---

[1] Qur'an 4:82 (SI)

[2] Paul Gwynne. *Buddha, Jesus, and Muhammad* (N.p.: WILEY Blackwell, 2014) 12.

[3] Ibid., 17.

from Ibn Ishaq in 750 CE.[4] The traditional views of Muhammad's life and the early years of

Islam are based exclusively on Muslim sources.[5] Specifically, the Koran, the Muslim biographies

of Muhammad, and the Hadith.[6] It is noteworthy that coins from the early years of Islam do not

mention Muhammed, leading some to speculate that his status may have been elevated by later

Muslims. [7]

The Constitution of Medina

This document is widely considered among scholars to be an authentic document from

the time of Muhammed.[8] It was made between Muhammed and the Jews of Medina and outlines

different rights.[9] It allowed Jews to retain their religious identity while still being incorporated as

part of Muhammed's rule.[10] This document partially shows the historicity of certain accounts in

the Qur'an, specifically the migration from Mecca to Medina and the agreement with the Jewish

tribes that were settled there. The document is also evidence that there were at least some written

texts in the time of Muhammed and that the society was not completely illiterate.

However, the differences between what is found in the Constitution of Medina and how it

is described in the hadith collections are noteworthy as Patricia Crone points out: "Whereas

written transmission exposed the document to a certain amount of weathering which it withstood

extremely well, oral transmission resulted in the disintegration of the text, the loss of the context

---

[4] Ibn Warraq, *Why I*, 66.

[5] Ibid.

[6] Ibid.

[7] Jeremy Johns. "Archaeology and the History of Early Islam: The First Seventy Years." *Journal of the Economic and Social History of the Orient* 46, no. 4 (2003): 414-416. https://doi.org/10.1163/156852003772914848

[8] Shoemaker, *Creating*, 129.

[9] Ibid.

[10] Ibid.

and a shift of the general meaning: the document which marked the foundation of the Prophet's polity has been reduced to a point about the special knowledge of the Prophet's cousin."[11]

The Future of Verifying Islamic Historicity

Cook and Crone summarize the current state regarding details of Islam's historicity: 'The historicity of the Islamic tradition is thus to some degree problematic; while there are no cogent internal grounds for rejecting it, there are equally no cogent external grounds for accepting it.'[12] Unfortunately, there is discouragement, if not outright prohibition, of archaeology in traditional Arabian environments such as the sites of the Mosque of the Haram at Mecca and the Mosque of the Prophet at Medina.[13] As Jeremy Johns puts it: "There is little prospect that archaeology will uncover new evidence of Islam from the first seventy years."[14]

Inconsistencies

Inconsistencies within the text can be a great way of showing possible errors. Inconsistencies will be used to describe possible instances of disagreement within the Qur'an.

Abrogation

When one initially looks at the Qur'an it is easy to see instances of inconsistencies. Although there are many examples, Muslims claim a doctrine called abrogation or *nasakh*. Abrogation is the concept that Allah has changed certain sections of the Qur'an in order to

---

[11] Patricia Crone. *Slaves on Horses: The Evolution of the Islamic Polity* (Cambridge: Cambridge University Press, 1980) 6. Quoted in Stephen J. Shoemaker. *Creating the Qur'an: A Historical-Critical Study* (N.p.: University of California Press, 2022) 200-201. https://www.amazon.com/Creating-Quran-Historical-Critical-Stephen-Shoemaker-ebook/dp/B0B13YBB27/ref=sr_1_1?crid=2OXZOIVD7JRKZ&keywords=creating+the+quran+shoemaker&qid=1694529213&s=books&sprefix=creating+the+quran+shoemaker%2Cstripbooks%2C148&sr=1-1

[12] Patricia Crone and Michael Cook. *Hagarism* (Cambridge University Press, 1977) 3. Quoted in M. R. Kazimi. *Revisionist History of Islam: A Critical Study of Post 1977 Interpretations* (Karach, Pakistan: SAMA, 2017) 25.

[13] Johns, "Archaeology," 433.

[14] Ibid., 411.

provide a better or more fitting command. As *Tafsir Ibn Kathir* elaborates: 'The Nasakh only occurs with commandments, prohibitions, permissions, and so forth. As for stories, they do not undergo Nasakh.'[15] *The Study Quran* explains: "As widely understood in the Islamic religious sciences, *naskh* can occur only in matters of commands and prohibitions, not in descriptive passages relating to metaphysics, ethics, history, the nature of God, or the Hereafter".[16] A verse could be abrogated due to certain commands only being applicable for a certain period of time and therefore a new command is given in order to be more appropriate for later circumstances. This is a concept that is often criticized. However, it does have similarities with other religions such as Christianity. For example, Christians believe that later covenants have replaced certain regulations placed on them such as dietary restrictions. Also, Abraham was told to sacrifice his son and then was told not to.[17]

Several verses reference abrogation in the Qur'an. Some of these verses seem to support the concept, while other verses seem to suggest that Allah's words cannot be changed. The former is seen in Q 2:106: "We do not abrogate a verse or cause it to be forgotten except that We bring forth [one] better than it or similar to it. Do you not know that Allāh is over all things competent?"[18] Q 16:101 reads: "And when We substitute a verse in place of a verse - and Allāh is most knowing of what He sends down - they say, 'You, [O Muḥammad], are but an inventor [of lies].' But most of them do not know."[19]

---

[15] Ibn Kathir. *Tafsir Ibn Kathir*. 2:106-107. Accessed using Quran.com.

[16] Seyyed H. Nasr, Caner K. Dagli, Maria M. Dakake, and Joseph E. Lumbard, eds. *The Study Quran: A New Translation and Commentary* (N.p: HarperCollins, 2015) 331, eBook. https://hcplc.bibliocommons.com/v2/record/S980C2123278.

[17] Ibn Kathir, *Tafsir*, 2:106-107.

[18] Qur'an 2:106 (SI)

[19] Qur'an 16:101 (SI)

It almost seems that the concept of abrogation itself was subjected to abrogation. This can be seen in conflicting verses such as Q 10:64: "For them are good tidings in the worldly life and in the Hereafter. No change is there in the words [i.e., decrees] of Allāh. That is what is the great attainment."[20] Similarly, in Q 6:115: "And the word of your Lord has been fulfilled in truth and in justice. None can alter His words, and He is the Hearing, the Knowing."[21] These verses seem to disallow abrogation and therefore are inconsistent with Q 2:106 and 16:101.

Certain items were believed to have existed at one time but were abrogated, and did not make it into the Qur'an such as the Valleys of Gold.[22] Sometimes verses stay in the Qur'an even though they're abrogated, and other times they are not included.[23] It is interesting to note that even though the Verse of Stoning was removed from the Qur'an it is still considered to be in effect.[24]

It is difficult to determine whether abrogation is a legitimate tool used by Allah to give more appropriate and time-specific instructions, or if this is a tool used by Muslim scholars to remedy instances in the Qur'an of clear inconsistencies. "According to Muir, some 200 verses have been canceled by later ones. Thus we have the strange situation where the entire Koran is recited as the word of God, and yet there are passages that can be considered not "true"; in other words, 3 percent of the Koran is acknowledged as falsehood."[25] Ibn Warraq comments:

> Now we can see how useful and convenient the doctrine of abrogation is in bailing scholars out of difficulties. Of course, it does pose problems for apologists of Islam, since

---

[20] Qur'an 10:64 (SI)

[21] Qur'an 6:115 (SI)

[22] Ibn Kathir, *Tafsir,* 2:106-107,

[23] Nasr et al., *The Study Quran,* 331-332.

[24] Ibid., 332.

[25] Ibn Warraq, *Why I,* 115.

all the passages preaching tolerance are found in Meccan, i.e., early suras, and all the passages recommending killing, decapitating, and maiming are Medinan, i.e., later: 'tolerance' has been abrogated by 'intolerance.' For example, the famous verse at sura 9.5, 'Slay the idolaters wherever you find them,' is said to have cancelled 124 verses that dictate toleration and patience.[26]

First-person Speech Other than by Allah

While texts, such as the Bible are considered "the word of God" even though others are speaking, when it comes to the Qur'an, it is literally considered the word of God because it is considered to be Allah who is speaking throughout the book. Sometimes Allah's speech can be given in the third person, however, it is still considered Allah speaking. There are instances in the Qur'an where other parties do talk, however this is differentiated from the speech of Allah. The problem is there are many instances in the Qur'an where other people are speaking without them being properly introduced as the speaker. This suggests to some critics that Muhammed may have been confused and created sections that were his speech, yet did not properly attribute the words to God. There are many instances in the Qur'an where the word "Say" is added before certain passages to explain why someone other than Allah is speaking. These are believed to be added by later editors according to some critics.[27]

Here are a few examples where the word "Say" may have been added, or instances where it is unlikely that Allah is the speaker. Q 27:91-92:

[Say, O Muḥammad], 'I have only been commanded to worship the Lord of this city, who made it sacred and to whom [belongs] all things. And I am commanded to be of the Muslims [i.e., those who submit to Allāh]. And to recite the Qur'ān.' And whoever is guided is only guided for [the benefit of] himself; and whoever strays - say, 'I am only [one] of the warners.'[28]

---

[26] Ibid.

[27] Ibid., 106.

[28] Qur'an 27:91-92 (SI)

Ibn Warraq adds: "As many have pointed out, one only needs to add the imperative 'say' at the beginning of the sura to remove the difficulty. This imperative form of the word "say" occurs some 350 times in the Koran, and it is obvious that this word has, in fact, been inserted by later compilers of the Koran, to remove countless similarly embarrassing difficulties."[29]

In another example, one can see sections where it is unlikely that Allah is speaking, such as when the Creation is described, and then immediately switches to what appears to be Muhammed speaking. This is evident as Muhammad describes himself as a "warner", as well as differentiating between himself and Allah: "And of all things We created two mates [i.e., counterparts]; perhaps you will remember. So flee to Allāh. Indeed, I am to you from Him a clear warner. And do not make [as equal] with Allāh another deity. Indeed, I am to you from Him a clear warner."[30]

The presence of first-person speech that appears not to be the words of Allah, but instead the words of Muhammad, is a possible refutation of the idea that the Qur'an is the actual words of God. There are many other examples within the Qur'an where this type of possible inconsistency is evident.

Commentaries (or *tafsirs*) on the Qur'an often do not mention the use of the first person by individuals other than Allah. In a rare instance, *Tafsir Ibn Kathir* does say this on Q 1:5: "We should mention that in this Ayah, the type of speech here changes from the third person to direct speech by using the Kaf in the statement Iyyaka (You). This is because after the servant praised and thanked Allah, he stands before Him, addressing Him directly".[31]

The lack of distinguishment between speakers in the Qur'an may be appropriate due to the poetic nature of the book. However, it does also seem that not only are there instances where

---

[29] Ibn Warraq, *Why I*, 106.

[30] Qur'an 51:49-51 (SI)

[31] Ibn Kathir, *Tafsir*, 1:5.

the words "say" or "pray" were added to the Qur'an to fix instances of speech other than by Allah, but also there appear to be instances where Muhammad is the speaker, possibly because he became confused or erred in communicating the revelations of Allah, in Allah's own words. This could be because of a few reasons: These revelations were not from Allah, there were issues when transcribing these revelations, or audiences do not fully understand when the speech was meant to be attributed to another party.

Does Allah Forgive Any Sin?

It is considered by many Muslims that the only sin that Allah will not forgive is the sin of *shirk*. *Shirk* is attributing deity to something or someone other than Allah. It is usually referenced concerning polytheists, especially those in Mecca at the time, and usually does not apply to followers of other Abrahamic religions such as Christianity or Judaism. The situation can be confusing, as certain commentaries on the Qur'an distinguish between whether it is meant that *shirk* cannot be forgiven without repentance, or cannot be forgiven at all.

These differing views can be seen in certain verses in the Qur'an: "Say, 'O My servants who have transgressed against themselves [by sinning], do not despair of the mercy of Allāh. Indeed, Allāh forgives all sins. Indeed, it is He who is the Forgiving, the Merciful.' "[32] In *Tafsir Ibn Kathir* it states that all sins can be forgiven as long as you repent.[33] Al-Jalalayn specifically includes idolatry as something that can be forgiven in his commentary on this verse.[34]

Q 4:116 appears to take a different view: "Indeed, Allāh does not forgive association with Him, but He forgives what is less than that for whom He wills. And he who associates others with Allāh has certainly gone far astray."[35] *Tafsir Ibn Kathir* appears to contradict its

---

[32] Qur'an 39:53 (SI)

[33] Ibn Kathir, *Tafsir*, 39:53-59.

[34] Jalal ad-Din Al-Maḥalli and Jalal ad-Din as-Suyuti. *Tafsīr al-Jalālayn*. (1505) 444.

[35] Qur'an 4:116 (SI)

commentary of verse 39:53 and says "Shirk Shall not be Forgiven", however, it is possible it means only if the sinner does not repent.[36] *The Study Quran* suggest that *shirk* will not be forgiven only if the individual dies unrepentant.[37]

So does Allah forgive all sins or does he forgive all sins except for *shirk*? It may be that any sin can be forgiven even if the sinner does not explicitly ask for repentance, with the exception of *shirk*. *Shirk* may require the sinner to explicitly ask for forgiveness for God to forgive it. However, this could be an instance of a possible inconsistency within the text.

Inaccuracies

Inaccuracies in a text are instances where the text of the Qur'an may differentiate from widely accepted facts. This could be an instance where the Qur'an conflicts with known information such as scientific facts.

Alexander the Great and Gog and Magog

There may be no instance more damning to the concept of Qur'anic inerrancy than the story of Alexander the Great and Gog and Magog. In the Islamic tradition, there are stories of Alexander the Great that are not found in any other respected historical documents. In one of these stories, Alexander the Great is described as building a great barrier between two mountains to imprison the people of Gog and Magog.

> They said, 'O Dhul-Qarnayn, indeed Gog and Magog are [great] corrupters in the land. So may we assign for you an expenditure that you might make between us and them a barrier?' He said, 'That in which my Lord has established me is better [than what you offer], but assist me with strength [i.e., manpower]; I will make between you and them a dam. Bring me bars of iron' - until, when he had leveled [them] between the two mountain walls, he said, 'Blow [with bellows],' until when he had made it [like] fire, he said, 'Bring me, that I may pour over it molten copper.' So they [i.e., Gog and Magog] were unable to pass over it, nor were they able [to effect] in it any penetration. [Dhul-Qarnayn] said, 'This is a mercy from my Lord; but when the promise of my Lord comes

---

[36] Ibn Kathir, *Tafsir*, 4:116.

[37] Nasr et al., *The Study Quran*, 945.

[i.e., approaches], He will make it level, and ever is the promise of my Lord true.' And We will leave them that day surging over each other, and [then] the Horn will be blown, and We will assemble them in [one] assembly.[38]

This story appears to be meant to be taken literally as can be seen from commentaries such as *Tafsir Ibn Kathir* and Al-Jalalayn.[39] Most commentators even believe that this event took place in the area of Armenia and Azerbaijan.[40] This is an issue because Muslims believe that Gog and Magog are still imprisoned to this day and will be released near the end of times. This is evident in Q 21:96: "Until when [the dam of] Gog and Magog has been opened and they, from every elevation, descend".[41]

The release of Gog and Magog is also taken literally, as evident in descriptions regarding their actions during "The Last Hour". There is even mention of Gog and Magog drinking all the water of a river likely due to their great numbers.[42] This is an issue for the concept of Qur'anic inerrancy. With modern satellite technology and topographical information, it is extremely unlikely that there is a group of people imprisoned behind a wall that has not been discovered today. It is also unlikely that after 2,000 years these people would not be able to breach this wall either by going over it, under it, or through it.

---

[38] Qur'an 18:94-99 (SI)

[39] Ibn Kathir, *Tafsir,* 18:92-96; Nasr et al., *The Study Quran,* 2977-2978.; *Tafsīr al-Jalālayn, 274.*

[40] Nasr et al., *The Study Quran,* 2978.

[41] Qur'an 21:96 (SI)

[42] Ibn Kathir, *Tafsir,* 21:95-97.

Prophecies

Muhammed is widely known as "The Prophet", however, he appears to have made very few prophecies, at least in the Qur'an. There are prophecies attributed to him in the hadith literature, which is briefly discussed below. When discussing prophecies one must differentiate between a failed prophecy and an unfulfilled prophecy. A failed prophecy is impossible to come true, whereas an unfulfilled prophecy has not yet come true. Many prophecies in both the Qur'an and the Bible are considered unfulfilled, and it is likely impossible to determine whether they are failed prophecies or ones that will come true in the future. Prophecies are a great way of looking at Qur'anic inerrancy, as an omniscient and omnipotent God should be able to make prophecies with 100% accuracy, assuming these prophecies are accurately recorded and passed down in the texts modern audiences have today.

Prophecies that are both given and fulfilled in the same book are hard to verify, and therefore I will try to avoid them here. Without external verification, a later editor can make these prophecies "true". Similarly, prophecies that do not have a substantial time gap between when they were given and when they were fulfilled are hard to verify.

Byzantine Victory

The most famous prophecy in the Qur'an and possibly all of Islam is the prophecy foretelling the victory of the Byzantines over the Persians. At the time it was given, it is believed that the Persians had just had a major victory over the Byzantines. Many believe that such a prophecy at this time was very unlikely to be fulfilled due to the poor tactical situation the Byzantines now found themselves in. This prophecy given by Muhammed predicts a future victory by the Byzantines in the following three to nine years.

Q 30:2-5: "The Byzantines have been defeated In the nearest land. But they, after their defeat, will overcome Within three to nine years. To Allāh belongs the command [i.e., decree] before and after. And that day the believers will rejoice".[43]

The Byzantines ended up having major victories over the Persians in the next few years. Eventually, the Byzantines defeated the Persians in a battle around 622 CE.[44] Many critics argue that no major victory was achieved within nine years of when the prophecy was believed to be given. However, Muslims refute this by saying that the initial victory around 622 CE was within the given time frame and that although this doesn't describe the ultimate victory at the Battle of Nineveh in 627[45], it was the initial victory in a series of triumphs that then led to their ultimate victory.[46] It is also questioned whether this prophecy was unlikely to happen given the Byzantines' situation. It may have been likely that at some point they would have victory over the Persians, and therefore this prophecy may not have been that "out on a limb".

This prophecy is also considered to have coincided with the Battle of Badr, a famous battle in Islamic history. Al-Jalalayn is one of those who believes that the Muslims learned of the Byzantines victory on the same day as the Battle of Badr.[47] Sometimes the reference to the believers rejoicing on that day does not only mean they are rejoicing due to the victory of the Byzantines because they believed in the same Abrahamic God, but also their own victory at the Battle of Badr.[48]

---

[43] Cite Qur'an 30:2-4 (SI)

[44] E. Franzius. "Heraclius." Encyclopedia Britannica, February 7, 2024. https://www.britannica.com/biography/Heraclius-Byzantine-emperor.

[45] Ibid.

[46] Nasr et al., *The Study Quran*, 3906.

[47] Maḥalli and as-Suyuti. *Tafsīr al-Jalālayn,* 383.

[48] Ibid.

It is also worth noting that there is a story in the hadith of Abu Bakr making a bet with some non-Muslims regarding this prophecy. It is believed that as per the terms of the bet, the timeline was set for the victory to occur within either five or six years.[49] However, after it did not occur in that time Abu Bakr lost the bet.[50] After this, the prophecy apparently did come true in the seventh year after it was made.[51]

Some believe that the word "nearest" in Q 30:3 can actually be translated as "lowest", bringing about a whole different set of prophetic implications with some people arguing that this shows that the Qur'an predicted that the Dead Sea area was the lowest point on earth a millennia before this was discovered by science.

Although there is debate regarding the fulfillment and difficulty of this prophecy, it does seem that this prophecy has no negative impact on the concept of Qur'anic inerrancy. There are questions regarding the Battle of Badr as occurring on the same day, however, with the information audiences have today this prophecy cannot be considered to have failed. However, the short time span between when it was given and fulfillment lead to questions of how authentic the prophecy is.

Hadith Prophecies

There are many more prophecies found in the hadith collections. These prophecies both appear to give evidence for and against the idea of inerrancy. However, this must be differentiated between hadith inerrancy and Qur'anic inerrancy, the latter being the focus of this book. As was stated earlier, if Qur'anic inerrancy is not tenable, it is unlikely that hadith inerrancy is tenable either. However, on the contrary, if the hadith literature is inerrant, at least

---

[49] Ibn Kathir, *Tafsir*, 30: 1-7.

[50] Ibid.

[51] Ibid.

those with a *sahih* designation, then this bodes well for Qur'anic inerrancy as criticism of the Qur'an's collection does not appear to be as intense compared to the hadiths. Also, if Hadith Science can accurately preserve information coming from the Prophet, then it is likely that the collections of Abu Bakr and Uthman were just as diligent.

Miracles

There are very few miracles described in the Qur'an, and there are many more examples of miracles in the hadith literature. There even appear to be instances in the Qur'an where Muhammed says that miracles will not be given because they will not change someone's mind regarding a belief in God. However, this seems to be inconsistent with other instances in the Qur'an, such as when Moses performed miracles in competition with Pharaoh's magicians.

Qur'an 7:117-121: "And We inspired to Moses, 'Throw your staff,' and at once it devoured what they were falsifying. So the truth was established, and abolished was what they were doing. And they [i.e., Pharaoh and his people] were overcome right there and became debased. And the magicians fell down in prostration [to Allāh]. They said, 'We have believed in the Lord of the worlds'".[52]

In this instance, it seems clear that the miracle performed by Moses changed the minds of the Egyptian magicians. *The Study Quran* comments that this was a "sincere submission to God".[53] This brings about questions of why Muhammed would not perform miracles, or his explanation that miracles would not change people's faith.

Splitting of the Moon

The splitting of the moon is considered one of the few, if not only, examples of Muhammad performing a physical miracle in the Qur'an. This is considered "by the vast

---

[52] Qur'an 7:117-121 (SI)

[53] Nasr et al., *The Study Quran,* 1783.

majority of commentators as a reference to a miracle performed by the Prophet."[54] In this story, Muhammed splits the moon for people as a sign.[55] *Tafsir Ibn Kathir* says: "it was among the clear miracles that Allah gave him".[56] This story is described in Q 54:1-2: "The Hour has come near, and the moon has split [in two]. And if they see a sign [i.e., miracle], they turn away and say, 'Passing magic.' "[57] *Tafsir* describe how Mount Hira was visible in between the two halves, suggesting that it was not just a minor, non-visible split in the moon.[58] It is also reported that there were even travelers they encountered days later who had witnessed the splitting of the moon, meaning that it was visible from other locations.[59]

This story is very hard to remedy with historical records as there does not appear to be any reliable source that describes this event. If the moon had split to the degree described in the Qur'an and other Islamic literature, then one would believe that this event should have been visible in a large part of the world. However, again there appear to be no reliable instances of this event being recorded among other civilizations of the day. The lack of historical evidence for such a visible and significant event leads to serious questions about the credibility of this account and therefore the inerrancy of the Qur'an.

Inimitability of the Qur'an

I'jaz, or the inimitability of the Qur'an, is often pointed to as the only true miracle given, and therefore has a subsequent impact on Muhammed's prophethood. The Qur'an's eloquence and poetic nature is considered to be so magnificent, due to the fact that it was written by Allah

---

[54] Ibid., 5132-5133.

[55] Ibn Kathir, *Tafsir*, 54:1-5.

[56] Ibid.

[57] Qur'an 54:1-2 (SI)

[58] Nasr et al., *The Study Quran*, 5133.

[59] Ibid.

himself, that it is believed to not be able to be imitated by anyone or anything. There are even instances in the Qur'an where the challenge is given for others to try to imitate the Qur'an, believing that they will inevitably fail. An example of this is Q 17:88: "Say, 'If mankind and the jinn gathered in order to produce the like of this Qur'ān, they could not produce the like of it, even if they were to each other assistants.' "[60]

Commentators believe that Muhammad's true miraculous gift was his poetry, especially when considering the belief that he was illiterate. This is in comparison to the gifts of other prophets such as the medical skills of Jesus and the magic of Moses.[61] *The Study Quran* explains that: "each messenger was sent with miracles".[62] *The Study Quran* also notes: "Muhammad was sent to the Arabs, whose major art form was poetry and eloquent speech, with a scripture whose literary and linguistic style was considered to be of unsurpassed beauty and power."[63]

These examples are hard to show in English due to the fact that most of the poetry, syntax, and rhymes are more evident in the Arabic translation of the Qur'an. However, critics of this suggest that this is a subjective test, and not able to be a true test of the miraculous nature of the Qur'an. Scholars such as Bell and Watt, point out the grammar and syntax errors within the Qur'an. Ibn Aṭīyah describes the inimitability of the Qur'an:

> The correct opinion and the one held by the majority of scholars in regard to the inimitability of the Qur'an is that it is due to the Qur'an's syntax and its veracity. This is because the Almighty's knowledge encompasses everything, and His knowledge encompasses all forms of discourse. Thus, in arranging the wording of the Qur'an, the Almighty knew exactly which word was best suited to follow the one before it, and which word best yielded the intended meaning. The Book of Allah is such that if a word were

---

[60] Qur'an 17:88 (SI)

[61] Sophia Vasalou and فاسالو صوفيا. "The Miraculous Eloquence of the Qur'an: General Trajectories and Individual Approaches / الاعجاز البلاغي للقرآن ـ اتجاهات هامة وآراء خاصة في دراساته." *Journal of Qur'anic Studies* 4, no. 2 (2002): 28. https://doi.org/10.3366/jqs.2002.4.2.23

[62] Nasr et al., *The Study Quran*, 1784.

[63] Ibid.

removed from it, and then the entire Arabic lexicon were searched for a better word, it would never be found.[64]

Summary

This chapter provides a sample of instances where the inerrancy of the Qur'an is examined. Further instances are available for study such as possible issues with cosmology, the story of Noah, and more. Instances that both attest and detract from Islam may also be found in the hadith collections. The above examples show that an objective reading of the Qur'an does not support the theory of Qur'anic inerrancy. While there is content that supports some aspects of the historicity of the Qur'an, errors can be seen in the form of inconsistencies and inaccuracies. This is especially evident in the case of Alexander the Great and Gog and Magog. Also, the lack of contemporary evidence for the splitting of the Moon does not bode well for Qur'anic inerrancy either.

---

[64] Al Imam, *Variant Readings*, xix.

CHAPTER 4

DOES INNERRANCY MATTER?

Many religious texts are considered "holy", "sacred", or "divinely inspired". What impact does the presence of errors in these texts have on the validity of their religion? Is inerrancy within a religion's holy text necessary for the authenticity or survival of a religion? Inerrancy does not seem to be required for the authenticity of a religion. However, what if the claim of inerrancy comes from a supreme being, especially one claimed to be omnipotent and omniscient, then this poses a more credible problem. How does one know that this "God" has claimed that the holy text sent down is inerrant unless it says so in the text in question? Moreover, what if the part of the scripture that claims it is inerrant is the part that contains the error?

In both Christianity and Islam, the claim that the Bible and the Qur'an respectively are inerrant is prevalent in both religions. These holy texts are not a perfect comparison considering the Bible was authored by many writers and the revelations of the Qur'an were only given to Muhammed. The Bible is seen as a collection of books compared to the Qur'an which is a single text. Also, the composition of the Bible occurred over many centuries compared to only a few decades in the case of the Qur'an. However, due to the belief in scriptural inerrancy in both Christianity and Islam, the Bible offers some parallels that help to better understand the theory of Qur'anic inerrancy.

The idea that it is possible for a holy text to contain errors but still contain divinely given truths is more common in Christianity than it is in Islam. In other words, the idea that the Qur'an is inerrant is much more widespread in Islam, with there being a seemingly small minority of Muslims who do not believe the Qur'an is perfect. Within both of these holy texts, some verses seem to suggest inerrancy. In Christianity, 2 Timothy 3:16 is often pointed to as proof that the Bible contains not a single mistake. 2 Timothy 3:16 reads: "All scripture is inspired by God and is useful for teaching, for reproof, for correction, and for training in righteousness".[1] As was stated above, this verse may be the one that is an error and is not necessarily proof that the entire Bible is without a single fault. Likewise, one could argue that this only refers to the inerrancy of 2 Timothy alone and not the entire Bible. Others argue that this verse does not necessarily claim biblical inerrancy and that the interpretation that it does include this belief, is not definitive.

Similar verses in the Qur'an also suggest this idea of inerrancy, such as Q 18:1-2: "[All] praise is [due] to Allāh, who has sent down upon His Servant [Muḥammad (ﷺ)] the Book and has not made therein any deviance. [He has made it] straight, to warn of severe punishment from Him and to give good tidings to the believers who do righteous deeds that they will have a good reward [i.e., Paradise]."[2] However, similarly to 2 Timothy 3:16, these verses may not explicitly state that the Qur'an is without error. Consequently, Qur'anic inerrancy may also be a matter of interpretation.

It is possible that the idea of Qur'anic inerrancy was never taught by Muhammad or Allah. One could argue that the story of the seven *ahruf* is evidence that Qur'anic inerrancy was never intended by Muhammad and is unnecessary for a proper faith in Islam. Similarly, the alleged story of the Prophet allowing changes to be made by his scribe may be an indicator that the Qur'an was never intended to be seen as inerrant. Qur'anic inerrancy may have been a later invention based on either an incorrect perception of the teachings of Muhammad, or maybe even have been due to the perceived necessity by later Muslims of safeguarding the text. However, while the early history of Islam is not crystal clear, and there are many questions regarding the accuracy of the accounts of the early years, many scholars agree they still represent a fair snapshot of the early history of Islam and Muhammed.

---

[1] 2 Timothy 3:16 (New Revised Standard Version Updated Edition).

[2] Qur'an 18:1-2 (SI)

One can imagine why a religion would want to claim inerrancy for its text, as even minor textual changes or interpretations could lead to drastic new ideas within the religion, and even new religions altogether. Depending on the changes, if one were to change even 1% of a holy scripture, it could have a massive impact on the major doctrines that the religion teaches, as well as the lives of its followers. One can see this in the many splinter religions that have come from Judaism, Christianity, Islam, and other religions. To most practicing Jews, Christianity is a splinter religion that mischaracterizes the messianic prophecies in a way that allows for Jesus to be seen as the awaited Messiah of the Hebrew scriptures. To many Christians, Mormonism is a mischaracterization of the history and major doctrines of Christianity. If biblical inerrancy is true, then the Mormon belief that Jesus was resurrected in the Americas is a much harder notion to make fit within the writings of the Bible.

In Islam, the Ahmadiyya movement claims that another Messiah came in the 1800s and has brought a new message from Allah. If one believes in the traditional Muslim view that Muhammad is the final prophet or the "Seal of the Prophets," then this movement is essentially impossible within the confines of Qur'anic inerrancy. However, once one claims that a holy text can contain errors, it opens up a Pandora's Box for possible manipulations and different interpretations of the mainstream perception of the text. Once one considers the different religions that have come from a "mother religion" it is easier to see why a religion's early followers may be more inclined to claim their scripture as inerrant. It is possible that a belief in inerrancy acts as a type of "guardrail", and that without it, the religion would eventually be altered, possibly beyond recognition, and may even fall victim to the depths of history.

However, the idea of inerrancy does not necessarily have to come because of a perceived threat to the religion by that religion's early followers. Most Christians or Muslims who believe in the inerrancy of the Bible or Qur'an respectively, truly believe this is a doctrine that is taught as part of their faith. It is nearly impossible to tell in modern times whether this belief comes from the teachings of the main individuals of their religion (e.g., Jesus, Muhammad, etc.), something that evolved later due to an incorrect interpretation by followers, or whether it was due to a tactical decision to preserve the integrity of the religion. Again, even if inerrancy is taught within the text, it does not necessarily mean that the text is an accurate depiction of what the "founders" of that religion intended.

If, however, one of the "founders" of Christianity or Islam did claim their scripture was inerrant and this could be definitively proven, and the holy text was found to contain mistakes, it would be devastating for that religion. For example, if Jesus who most Christians believe to be an omnipotent and omniscient God, truly taught that the Bible was inerrant, and it was also proven that the Bible had been perfectly preserved until modern times. Then, the presence of errors within the Bible would be horrific for the future of Christianity as a religion. Similarly, if the idea of Qur'anic inerrancy was revealed to Muhammed from an omnipotent and omniscient God, and if Muhammad accurately transcribed the words of that God through the Angel Gabriel, and if the process of the collection of the Qur'an was also without errors. Then, any error found in the Qur'an would be devastating for the perceived validity of the Qur'an and therefore the religion of Islam. However, one cannot definitively say that the words modern audiences have of the Bible or the Qur'an have been accurately and perfectly preserved since the "founding fathers" of their respective religions. Even if one could, he or she cannot definitively claim that the "founders" taught scriptural inerrancy, as one can argue that the verses within the Bible and the Qur'an that are often pointed to in order to prove inerrancy, are not without the ability to be interpreted in different ways.

Addressing Allegory and Relativism

One should not confuse inerrancy with absolute literalism. Holy texts often contain allegorical stories that were not intended to be interpreted literally. Most Christians would not consider many of Jesus's parables to describe historical events but instead are fictitious stories used to teach a lesson or idea. However, allegorical and metaphorical interpretations are often used as an excuse for possible errors in a holy text. Determining when a portion of a text is to be interpreted allegorically compared to when it contains a genuine error is not always easy.

Some people uphold relativism and the extreme skepticism that comes with it. They might claim that one really cannot know anything with certainty. These individuals may also claim that when it comes to a text written by an omnipotent and omniscient being, mere mortals cannot identify a perceived error within the text. They would claim that in reality, the perceived error is true. However, humans do not have significant intelligence in comparison to a supreme being and cannot understand the truth of that portion of the text. This is an understandable argument, however, one that is almost certainly impossible to debate. If something that looks like an objective clear-cut mistake, however in the mind of a perfect divine being is not an error, then this opens up another Pandora's Box of implications for humanity. If something appears to be undoubtedly wrong or undoubtedly right, but in reality, humanity has no way to determine the difference, then how can one ever live a moral life or ever be expected to make correct and righteous decisions? If one were to take this to its extreme one could argue that acts that almost all of humanity and most major religions see as morally abhorrent such as murder, rape, and torture now become debatable. One of these extreme skeptics could argue that it is possible that these acts are correct in the mind of a divine being, and that they only seem morally wrong due to the limits of the wisdom of human beings.

For the sake of argument and rational discourse, one must set this type of extreme skepticism aside when discussing the inerrancy of the Qur'an. In other words, while it is possible that something that is an objective and clear mistake in a holy text, could somehow in the mind of a perfect omnipotent omniscient being, be the truth, one must assume humans can determine between truth and falsehood at least on some level. Otherwise, one can make the argument that not a single word found in any religious text could ever be properly interpreted or understood by a human, and therefore is either useless to read or could have an infinite number of interpretations, none of which could ever be proven or possibly even understood by humanity. In other words, for the sake of argument and any common agreement among humanity, one must assume that if a text says something like "Thou shall not murder" this is not some abstract idea that has nothing to do with one human killing another human, but an understandable and discernible principle.

Religion vs Mythology

When does an ideology stop being described as religion and become relegated to the status of mythology? The amount of errors within a religion's stories and narratives does seem to have a massive impact on its widespread acceptance. [3] At some point, it does seem that if the stories associated with the religion contain unbelievable or objectively false information, the religion will not be accepted by the mainstream. Very few people on this planet still believe in Zeus, Poseidon, Thor, or Odin. It is extremely uncommon for someone to say: "Well I don't believe that Zeus came down and had sex with someone as an animal; but I still believe in Zeus, and that he and the other gods are up on Mount Olympus." At some point, it does seem that the amount of truth compared to perceived errors in a religious tradition does impact not only its mainstream acceptability but also its survival as a culturally accepted religion. [4] It is likely much easier for an employee who is a practicing Jew to get a Saturday off work, than for another employee who asks for a day off for a widely unknown Norse holiday. [5] While an individual can

---

[3] Factors such as failed prophecy can hurt the survivability of a religion. However, failed prophecy does not always lead to the end of a religion. See Stuart A. Wright, Michael Stausberg, and Carole M. Cusack, "How Religions End: Terms and Types," in Michael Stausberg, Stuart A. Wright, and Carole M. Cusack, eds. *The Demise of Religion: How Religions End, Die, or Dissipate* (London: Bloomsbury Academic, 2020) 20-21.

[4] Or at least its survival without major changes to the religion's original form.

[5] Minority religions are often cast as a threat to the public. See Wright, Stausberg, and Cusack, "How Religions End: Terms and Types," 23.

believe in a religion that has established traditions that contain significant errors, this does not seem to be the case on a long-term widespread societal level.

This brings up the role inerrancy plays in terms of a nation's or society's acceptance of a religion. [6] The level of acceptance on a broader societal level seems to have a major influence on the acceptance of these religions on an academic level. It is no secret that the level of discretion and sensitivity that is afforded to major world religions such as Christianity and Islam are not equal to what is afforded to what is perceived as mythology. When discussing major world religions it seems that one must be more careful not to offend others than if one were to be discussing the beliefs of ancient Egypt or a similar "dead" religion. It appears that inerrancy, or at least the number of errors in a religious tradition, plays a major role in not only its acceptance contemporarily but also its longevity as a widely respected religion. It seems that if a religion does contain too many unbelievable stories or too many false facts (such as scientific facts or failed prophecies), given enough time, this religion will be downgraded to the status of mythology.

Final Thoughts

Often many holy texts of major religions are seen as literary works of art and are an important part of history. This is undoubtedly true, and regardless of the validity of the religion, the text is invaluable for understanding humanity. There is also the argument that these books represent a type of moral theory that is widely adapted and arguably indispensable for even

---

[6] The state plays an active role in the relative success or failure of a religion. See Michael Stausberg, "Introduction: The Demise of Religions: or Do Religions End?" in Stausberg, Michael, Stuart A. Wright, and Carole M. Cusack, eds. *The Demise of Religion: How Religions End, Die, or Dissipate* (London: Bloomsbury Academic, 2020). 10.; Sometimes raids by a state government have led to the dissolution or destruction of a religion. See Wright, Stausberg, and Cusack, "How Religions End: Terms and Types," 24.; In France, a state agency has been set up to monitor cults and sects. See Stuart A. Wright, "State Actions in Western Democracies Leading to the Dissolution of Religious Communities," in Stausberg, Michael, Stuart A. Wright, and Carole M. Cusack, eds. *The Demise of Religion: How Religions End, Die, or Dissipate* (London: Bloomsbury Academic, 2020) 167-168.; Repression by the state does not always negatively affect a religion. It can sometimes lead to an increase in membership.

modern audiences. These books indeed contain many lessons that should be implemented across the globe such as not to murder, steal, or rape. The argument that arises is whether these books captured objective truths that have been realized by humanity without divine guidance and passed down through history, or whether these modern objective views of morality have been widely accepted due to them being passed down from a supreme being (often claimed to be recorded and passed down in a holy text).

It must also be noted that these texts often contain teachings such as the inferiority of women, homophobia, and other lessons that are not widely accepted in modern society. How does one decide which of these are truths and which of these are errors? One must find the proper balance between respect for different cultures and supporting illogical viewpoints.[7] As Leonard Binder says: "Tolerance has nowhere more exceeded its own scope than in the contemporary liberal attitude toward religion."[8]

The acceptance of the LGBT+ community has appeared to have increased among Christians in the last few decades. One could argue that there is a similar trend regarding the acceptance of the equality of women by both Christians and Muslims. While many of these trends are likely due to new and more progressive interpretations of their respective holy texts, it is also likely due to an increased percentage of members of these faith traditions no longer believing that their holy book is inerrant. This is just one example of the effect that changing views on inerrancy can have on a religion as well as the values and ideology that it teaches.[9]

---

[7] Richard Dawkins talks about something similar in his book *The God Delusion* (p.42-50)

[8] Binder, *Islamic Liberalism*, 2.

[9] One study found that 88% of male Muslims and 86% of female Muslims denounced homosexuality as forbidden by Islamic law or scripture. Most participants cited the Qur'an or hadiths as the primary source of homonegative and heterosexist views. See Golshan Golriz. "Does Religion Prevent LGBTQ Acceptance? A Case Study with Queer and Trans Muslims in Toronto, Canada." Journal of Homosexuality 68, no. 14 (n.d.): 2453. http://dx.doi.org/10.1080/00918369.2020.1809888.

The belief in inerrancy and the amount of errors in a holy text seem to have a major impact on factors such as: the interpretation of a holy text, the limitation on the changes to doctrine, the ability to accommodate new contemporary viewpoints, the rise of splinter religions, the number of adherents across the globe, a religion's longevity in the course of history, and a religion's wide-spread social acceptance.[10]

---

[10] Further research is required to fully understand the role scriptural inerrancy and the perceived amount of errors in a holy text have on the rise of splinter religions, limiting changes to a religion's doctrine, a religion's longevity, societal acceptance of a religion, wide-spread adherence to a religion, as well as other areas.; There is little scholarship that explores the causes of how religions end. See Wright, Stausberg, and Cusack, "How Religions End: Terms and Types," 13.

CONCLUSION

There are many questions regarding the concept of Qur'anic inerrancy. This can be seen in the seemingly contradictory claims found in the historic Islamic account of the collection of the Qur'an. Not only does this account appear to be a combination of multiple incompatible accounts, but even the combined account appears to have quite a few illogical steps within its narrative. This also applies to the argument that Muhammed compiled the text of the Qur'an in his lifetime as this does not seem to work with Zaid's reluctance to do what Muhammad did not do.[1] Nor does it seem to work with the collection being a result of the death of those who memorized the Qur'an at the battle of Yamama. Even if the text had been compiled in some great part while Muhammad was still alive, there are still questions, such as the reasoning for asking everyday people to bring revelations. It also does not seem to make sense for Uthman to recompile the Qur'an after Abu Bakr. Of course, Muslim scholars have arguments for most, if not all of these perceived incompatibilities, but these arguments seem lacking.

There are also questions as to whether the theory of Qur'anic inerrancy is reasonable in light of the late standardization of vowel markings. These vowel markings were standardized centuries after Uthman's codex, and different vowel markings can produce different words. While context likely allows for determining an appropriate word in most circumstances, this is unlikely in all situations. As Al-Imam stated: "justification for substituting any of the Qur'an's words with their synonyms is completely unacceptable."[2]

---

[1] Al-Bukhari, *Sahih*, 4986. Quoted in Al-Azami, *The History*, 78.

[2] Al Imam, *Variant Readings*, xxi.

Another area that affects the concept of Qur'anic inerrancy is the seven different versions also known as the seven *ahruf*. This explanation allows for the different variants that occurred, even those immediately after Uthman, including the codices copied directly from his standardized text. The argument for this from a Muslim point of view is that they each *harf* reveals an approved variant. The claim of the seven *ahruf* strains logical sense.[3] One may ask whether the variations in these texts were actually known and approved by Muhammed, or were these differences something that occurred in the first few years of Islam before there was a standardized text.[4] However, to most Muslims the modern Qur'an cannot contain even a single mistake because of Qur'an 15:9: "Indeed, it is We who sent down the message [i.e., the Qur'ān], and indeed, We will be its guardian."[5]

As I examined historical views of inerrancy within Islamic scholarship, one can see that even many noncanonical manuscripts exist from the time of early Islam and the centuries after. Also, important figures appeared to endorse different noncanonical versions of the Qur'anic text. These figures include Ibn Masud and Ubayy Ka'b, as both of these individuals were considered some of the best in terms of their expertise on the Qur'an. This does not mean that these manuscripts necessarily reflected the common understanding at the time or that the possession of these variants by notable Muslim scholars reflects an endorsement of their validity. However, their presence raises serious questions about the agreement on the standardization of Uthman's

---

[3] Further research would be useful to determine if variants within the copies of the original Uthmanic codices and other accepted variants, can be considered to have numbered seven.

[4] Mattson, *The Story*, 96-97.

[5] Mattson, *The Story*, 96-97.; Qur'an 15:9 (SI)

Qur'anic text that has come down to modern audiences. This is in addition to other facts, such as the Dome of the Rock having a noncanonical verse on its inscription, as well as coins from this era having variant texts as well. It seems that the traditional Islamic account may not describe the events as accurately as they happened. Much of this information suggests that the standardization of Uthman's Qur'an was not as instantaneous or as unanimous as many Muslim scholars like to suggest.

In Chapter Three, I looked at possible examples of errors within the Qur'anic texts. These took a variety of different forms. While there were instances of accuracy, such as the Constitution of Medina, there were also instances of what appeared to be mistakes. The story of Alexander the Great and Gog and Magog may be one of the most damaging notions to the theory of Qur'anic inerrancy. The references seem to suggest that Gog and Magog are still currently walled up somewhere on Earth. These imprisoned people have not been discovered with modern-day satellite imagery. Also, the lack of historical accounts for something as extraordinary as the splitting of the moon leaves questions as to the inerrancy of the Qur'an. At the very least it brings great questions into how literally one can read the text of the Qur'an. It is possible that if one is to take an allegorical or metaphorical position many of these perceived errors may be remedied. This brings the question of whether an allegorical interpretation is the true interpretation, or whether it is an inappropriate human effort used to preserve the concept of inerrancy. The question of literal versus allegorical interpretations of the Qur'an is a debate that exists today.

The concept of abrogation seems like a tool used to explain what are clear inconsistencies within the Qur'an. Patrick Madigan summarizes Louay Fatoohi's findings on abrogation: "It is a later invention, devised by embarrassed legal scholars, and read back into the original corpus of laws to allow judges to achieve coherence in their pronouncements."[6] He goes on: "this was a form of deception or deceit practiced from the very beginning to allow Islam to escape the charge of contradiction in its most basic, authoritative documents".[7]

Qur'anic inerrancy does seem to fair better than biblical inerrancy. However, the Qur'an is notably shorter than the Bible. If the Qur'an were longer it is possible that more mistakes would occur. Similarly, the presence of the Gospels in the New Testament allows for four separate substantial accounts of the same events. While the Qur'an does also have instances where separate sections describe the same event, these are not nearly as lengthy and detailed as what is found in the Gospels. When comparing accounts of the same event it would likely be easier to find inconsistent information. Therefore, while the Qur'an may indeed be a text that is a more accurate preservation of a divinely inspired message, it could also be that the Bible is in more of a position to reveal possible errors due to its length and organization.

This brings one to the question: Does inerrancy matter? It could be argued that Muhammad never intended the Qur'an to be considered inerrant in any modern understanding of the word. This may be seen in the concept of the seven *ahruf* as well as the story of Muhammad allowing his scribe to alter phrases in the Qur'an.

The Qur'an is believed to be a correction of earlier corrupted texts such as the Bible. If earlier texts were allowed to be corrupted why are Muslims so confident that the Qur'an is

---

[6] Patrick Madigan. "Abrogation in the Qur'an and Islamic Law: A Critical Study of the Concept of 'naskh' and Its Impact. by Louay Fatoohi. Pp. Xiv, 287, Ny/Milton Park, Routledge, 2014, £80.00." *Heythrop Journal* 57, no. 1 (2016): 251. https://doi.org/10.1111/heyj.120_12307.

[7] Ibid.

immune? Compared to biblical literature the Qur'an seems to have a better argument that its contemporary contents are more accurately preserved. However, while there are many Muslim arguments for the different perceived issues related to the theory of Qur'anic inerrancy, it seems massively unlikely that all of these independent issues are explainable, and that all break in favor of Qur'anic inerrancy.

This book examined the background and topics associated with the theory of Qur'anic inerrancy. After examining the evidence, while the text of the Qur'an probably offers a solid understanding of the words and beliefs of Muhammad, it appears to contain errors. It seems that from an objective point of view, it is extremely unlikely that the text of the Qur'an is inerrant. Shoemaker summarizes:

> Given the dynamics of oral tradition, as well as its limitations and regular distortions, searching for the original words of Muhammad is clearly a fool's errand. It is utterly implausible, not to say impossible, that we have them. Again, unless his teachings were taken down under his supervision while he was alive, which is not in evidence, to imagine that we today have the words of Muhammad in the Qur'an is either an act of religious faith, in the case of the devout Muslim, or a delusion, in the case of the modern historian. At best we can expect to find in the Qur'an some of the basic gist of what Muhammad taught his followers, as these teachings were remembered and retold again and again by his followers within this sectarian milieu of the late ancient Near East.[8]

This book also analyzed the potential effects of errant scriptures on the associated religion. While further research is needed to confirm the theories presented in Chapter Four, it appears that perceived errors in sacred texts may have a significant impact on the social acceptance of the associated religion. This includes factors such as: the interpretation of a holy text, the limitation on the changes to doctrine, the ability to accommodate new contemporary

---

[8] Shoemaker, *Creating*, 195.

viewpoints, the rise of splinter religions, the number of adherents across the globe, a religion's longevity in the course of history, and a religion's wide-spread social acceptance.

Even if the Qur'an is not inerrant or perfectly preserved, it does not necessarily reflect that Muhammad was not a prophet who received revelations from an omnipotent omniscient God. One must note the difference between the theory of Qur'anic inerrancy and the concept that Muhammad's revelations are actually from Allah.[9] In the final section, I will briefly discuss the role of reason and faith in relation to errant holy texts and their respective religions.

How Big of a "Leap"?

What is the relationship between logic and faith when believing in a religion? For most major religions, especially the major Abrahamic religions, the major tenets of their faith have been passed down through some type of holy text. If a religion's holy texts do indeed contain errors then what effect does this have on the perceived validity of that religion?

There is a level of circular reasoning in using a holy text to argue one's religion, while simultaneously claiming faith is needed to believe in that religion's holy text. This issue is compounded when one abandons the notion of inerrancy. Why should someone believe a religion provides universal truths in a book that is not entirely true? If a witness goes on the stand and gives testimony, and parts of that testimony are found to be false, at a certain point one will likely question the overall testimony of that witness.

Even Christians, who believe that Jesus was the son of God, but do not believe the Bible is inerrant, will likely agree that if a description of an event contains too many errors then at

---

[9] Brubaker, *Corrections*, xxiv.

some point one should question the entirety of that description. The number of errors that can be tolerated before a text, account, or other description's major principles are questioned is subjective and dependent on each person. For some people the testimony must be 99% accurate, for some it's 75%, and for others, it's 50%. For some, a book such as the Bible or the Qur'an could be full of non-historical events, people, and places and yet still contain paramount truths that allow for the religion as a whole to be believable. The number of errors that can be tolerated before belief is rejected is dependent on each individual person.

An individual should also ask themselves what should come first: faith or evidence? Does faith (often taught from childhood) allow someone to believe in a text, that if it were outside of their religion, they would not afford the same degree of error to be present? Often individuals of a religion do not impose the same level of acceptability and skepticism on their own beliefs, as beliefs outside their religion. Each person must decide if they are willing to look at their religion from an objective point of view.

Does the presence and the degree of error within a holy text affect the believability and validity of the associated religion? Does religious revisionism make sense? George Ernest Wright comments: "In Biblical faith, everything depends upon whether the central events actually occurred."[10] Roland de Vaux adds: "if the historical faith of Israel is not founded in history, such faith is erroneous, and therefore, our faith is also."[11] As William G. Dever wrote:

---

[10] William G. Dever. *What Did the Biblical Writers Know & When Did They Know It?: What Archaeology Can Tell Us about the Reality of Ancient Israel* (Grand Rapids: William B. Eerdmans Publishing Company, 2001) 21.

[11] Israel Finkelstein and Neil Asher Silberman. *The Bible Unearthed: Archaeology's New Vision of Ancient Israel and the Origin of the Sacred Texts* (New York: Simon and Schuster, 2001) 34.

"Is such a Bible, stripped of its essential proclamation of 'God who acts in history,' not robbed of all its religious power and moral meaning?"[12]

It seems there are four options.[13] 1) Accept scriptural inerrancy and fundamentalism, which Dever believes is "oblivious to any critical thinking."[14] 2) Accept both faith and new critical methods, including new archaeological assessments. This is essentially trying to find a way for both religious texts and modern scientific findings to coexist.[15] 3) See religious texts as 'history-like'.[16] In other words, sacred texts do not have to be entirely true to still contain significant truths that pertain to the human experience.[17] 4) Reject religious texts and their associated religions.[18]

Mark Allan Powell, a Christian, seems to take the third option:

> The story is grounded in history, but, for me, the authenticity (or 'truth') of the story does not ultimately depend on the historicity of every aspect or detail. If one asks *how much* of the story—or *which aspects* of the story—must be historically accurate (or even historically verifiable) for the story to remain trustworthy and true,... I have no good answer. That would be a *theological* question or even a *spiritual* question; it is something that I think about from time to time, but I have never been able to answer. I am sure that

---

[12] Dever. *What Did*, 281.

[13] William G. Dever. *The Lives of Ordinary People in Ancient Israel: Where Archaeology and the Bible Intersect* (Grand Rapids: William B. Eerdmans Publishing Company, 2012) 380.

of 380

[14] Ibid.

[15] Ibid.

[16] Hans Frei. *The Eclipse of the Biblical Narrative: A Study in Eighteenth and Nineteenth Century Hermeneutics* (New Haven: Yale University Press, 1974) Quoted in William G. Dever. *The Lives of Ordinary People in Ancient Israel: Where Archaeology and the Bible Intersect* (Grand Rapids: William B. Eerdmans Publishing Company, 2012) 380.

[17] Dever, *The Lives*, 380.

[18] Ibid.

there is a line somewhere, a point at which if I became convinced the story lacked historical viability I would have to regard it as a falsehood, as a story to be rejected—or, at least, as a tale to be valued only for its charm, values, and symbolism. I am not certain where that line might be.[19]

These statements also apply to the Qur'an, and therefore Islam. The question is even if not every detail is correct, are the major tenets still true? Does the book accurately portray God's wisdom? Often it is said: "you must take a leap of faith" or "faith is a virtue". Faith seems necessary in any religion, but how big of a leap does God expect someone to take? Why should God expect someone to be rational, and not naïve, in other non-religious areas of life, but to suspend that when it comes to one's religion? What if one applied this same degree of faith to other aspects of life, such as a performance by an illusionist, or an "African prince" who emails asking for money? There are likely to be many things one does not understand compared to an omniscient and omnipotent supreme being. However, if God has given humanity logic and rational thought, it seems that He would want them to use it. Even if faith is required, should it not still be based on evidence? Would not a true religion have more evidence and therefore require less of a "leap" than a false one? Solomon Schimmel adds:

> Moreover, from this perspective, the laws and other norms that God revealed should in principle conform to reason, because reason is a characteristic of God, and so his teachings and commandments cannot be irrational. In addition, divine teachings and assertions about nature and history must be true, because truthfulness is another of God's characteristics. Because God endowed humans with the unique capacity to reason it is plausible to assume that he would want humans to exercise that capacity as they contemplated his laws and submitted to them. Not only should his laws be compatible with reason, but divine utterances about reality should be true. Would God endow me with reason and then ask me to believe in things that are unreasonable or false, or ask me to engage in irrational behaviors? Surely not."[20]

---

[19] Mark A. Powell. *Jesus as a Figure in History: How Modern Historians View the Man from Galilee*. 2nd Ed. (Louisville: Westminster John Knox Press, 2013). 9.

[20] Schimmel, *The Tenacity*, 20.

Does not the matter of whether a religious text is true or not directly relate to whether the religion it describes is true as well? A holy text may be able to contain errors, but at some point, too many errors should give audiences great concern about whether the associated religion is truly the teachings of a supreme being. Similarly, if a religious tradition has said that its religious text is inerrant from its earliest history, if the text contains mistakes, should one not then at least question that religion's traditions?

Also, what is the burden of proof? Does something have to be beyond reasonable doubt or a preponderance of the evidence? This is compounded when considering the gravity of eternity, especially the concept of hell, a concept that is taught in many religions. Does it make sense that there is not more overwhelming evidence compared to the level of consequence? "As Anthony Flew remarked there is an inordinate disparity between finite offenses and infinite punishments."[21]

Scriptural inerrancy does not appear to be necessary for any religion. It may not even have been intended by early founders. However, one must ask how these concepts made their way into their respective religious traditions. Is it because this is an incorrect doctrine of a true faith? Or is it the canary in the coal mine? Every believer will have to decide for themselves how many errors should be present in a text from God before they start to question if maybe their holy text has a more mortal source.

There is very little scholarship that deals specifically with Qur'anic inerrancy. This

has aimed to fill that gap by giving an overview of the theory of Qur'anic inerrancy and the topics that influence it. Also, I have theorized on the possible connection between scriptural inerrancy and a multitude of factors such as wide-spread societal acceptance and the likelihood of splinter religions. Future research could be aimed at topics such as the relation between the copies made from Uthman's codex (and other accepted variant texts) and the concept of the

[21] Ibn Warraq, *Why I*, 126.

seven *ahruf*. Further examples within the Qur'an that either support or detract from Qur'anic inerrancy could also provide insight. Also, I recommend further study into the possible connection between errors in scripture and a religion's long-term sustainability and social acceptance.

www.ingramcontent.com/pod-product-compliance
Lightning Source LLC
LaVergne TN
LVHW010653200726

843507LV00011B/1848